125 best
Microwave Oven recipes

Johanna Burkhard

Robert
ROSE

125 Best Microwave Oven Recipes
Text copyright © 2004 Johanna Burkhard
Photographs copyright © 2004 Robert Rose Inc.

For complete cataloguing information, see page 185.

Disclaimer
The recipes in this book have been carefully tested by our kitchen and our tasters. To the best of our knowledge, they are safe and nutritious for ordinary use and users. For those people with food or other allergies, or who have special food requirements or health issues, please read the suggested contents of each recipe carefully and determine whether or not they may create a problem for you. All recipes are used at the risk of the consumer. Consumers should always consult their microwave oven manufacturer's manual for recommended procedures and cooking times.

We cannot be responsible for any hazards, loss or damage that may occur as a result of any recipe use.

For those with special needs, allergies, requirements or health problems, in the event of any doubt, please contact your medical advisor prior to the use of any recipe.

Design & Production: PageWave Graphics Inc.
Photography: Mark T. Shapiro
Editor: Carol Sherman
Recipe Tester: Jennifer MacKenzie
Copy Editor: Julia Armstrong
Food Styling: Kate Bush
Prop Styling: Charlene Erricson
Color Scans & Film: Rayment & Collins / Colour Technologies

Cover image: Singapore Noodles with Chicken (page 60)

The publisher and author wish to express their appreciation to the following suppliers of props used in the food photography:

DISHES, LINENS AND ACCESSORIES
Homefront
371 Eglinton Avenue West
Toronto, Ontario M5N 1A3
Tel: (416) 488-3189
www.homefrontshop.com

FLATWARE
Gourmet Settings Inc.
245 West Beaver Creek Road, Unit 10
Richmond Hill, Ontario L4B 1L1
Tel: 1-800-551-2649
www.gourmetsettings.com

We acknowledge the financial support of the Government of Canada through the Book Publishing Industry Development Program (BPIDP) for our publishing activities.

Published by Robert Rose Inc.
120 Eglinton Avenue East, Suite 800, Toronto, Ontario, Canada M4P 1E2
Tel: (416) 322-6552 Fax: (416) 322-6936

Printed in Canada

1 2 3 4 5 6 7 8 9 CPL 12 11 10 09 08 07 06 05 04

Contents

Acknowledgments

I FEEL VERY FORTUNATE to have so many talented colleagues, friends and family who helped shape this book. First, I'd like to thank my publisher Bob Dees. This book came to life in a conversation with him about the need for an up-to-date collection of microwave recipes for today's kitchens. Having written a newspaper column about microwave cooking for eight years, I felt a fresh approach to this topic would be of interest to home cooks. He wholeheartedly agreed and made this book a reality.

I wish to thank my kitchen assistants — my daughter Nicole, and Penny Kaczmarek — for their expert help in preparing and testing recipes, as well to Jennifer MacKenzie for her thorough reviewing and retesting of recipes.

A very special thanks to Carol Sherman, a superb editor, who put the book together so efficiently, and to copy editor Julia Armstrong. Also, to the creative production team at PageWave Graphics — Andrew Smith, Joseph Gisini, Kevin Cockburn and Daniella Zanchetta — for the terrific book design and layout; to food stylist Kate Bush, food photographer Mark Shapiro and prop stylist Charlene Ericson for the beautiful photos; and to Marian Jarkovich at Robert Rose for her assistance in marketing and promotion.

My appreciation to Jimmy Chang, Senior Marketing Manager, Panasonic Canada Inc. for his technical advice regarding microwave ovens.

A grateful thanks to Norm Beal and my colleagues at Peninsula Ridge Estates Winery for their continued support and encouragement in my cookbook projects.

To my family and friends, whose caring, guidance and support are always so much appreciated — a heartfelt thanks.

And finally to my children, Nicole and Patrick, who share my enthusiasm and passion for cooking — a loving thanks for all of the wonderful moments together in the kitchen!

Introduction

I LOVE MY MICROWAVE oven. I couldn't live without it. I wrote this cookbook so everyone could come to appreciate their microwave like I do mine.

A microwave is a cook's best friend and has become the most-beloved appliance in the kitchen. More than 90 per cent of North American households now have one.

When microwaves debuted more than 35 years ago, it was predicted that they would revolutionize our kitchens and how we cooked. They did not live up to that lofty expectation. Supposedly, we would prepare complete gourmet meals in our microwave ovens but lifestyle trends have changed since then to reflect a simpler way of cooking. Unfortunately, that means today's cooks use their microwaves, for the most part, to defrost, reheat and make popcorn. That's a shame. My aim is to actually get you to cook in them.

With new automated features and the debut of second-generation microwaves that are lighter and less cumbersome, these appliances offer a wider range of cooking possibilities than ever before.

My aim in writing the *125 Best Microwave Oven Recipes* cookbook is not to get you to revamp your cooking style but rather to help you make better use of your microwave oven. If you only use your microwave for a few basic tasks, then perhaps it's time to reconsider how you're using the appliance in your kitchen. Designed to alter the stereotype that the microwave is only useful for defrosting and reheating, The *125 Best Microwave Oven Recipes* cookbook highlights dishes and techniques the microwave oven does best. Whether it is to make a speedy meal-in-one casserole, to replicate a slow cooker when simmering stews, or to use in tandem with your conventional oven, stovetop or grill, this reliable appliance helps reduce the time it takes to make tasty, nourishing meals.

In today's busy households, dinner often plays second fiddle to juggling work schedules, family commitments and a host of activities that demand our time. Yet suppers need to be appetizing and nutritious. With our hectic schedules and frantic pace, it's almost impossible to make a meal from scratch every night. Who has the time anymore?

If daunted by the daily task of getting supper on the table, the *125 Best Microwave Oven Recipes* cookbook offers a collection of recipes for fast and tasty meals. Many of these quick dishes are personal favorites I rely on. I've included plenty of easy grain, rice and pasta options — such as *Potato and Chickpea Chili*, *Risotto with Parmesan*, and *Chicken Penne Casserole with Broccoli* — that are a breeze to make.

Helpful hints to speed preparation accompany many of the recipes in this book. I have focused on dishes that require little stirring or attention, or those that can be prepared in a single casserole for easy cleanup, such as *Spicy Asian Beef with Peppers and Snow Peas*, *Creole Chicken and Rice Bake*, and *Spanish Fish Stew*.

Many of the recipes rely on timesaving convenience products found in supermarkets. To help cope with the six o'clock rush, I count on canned stock, pasta-ready tomato sauces, assorted canned beans such as kidney and black beans, salsas, preshredded cheeses, the new assortment of frozen vegetables and ready-cut vegetables. All of them come to the rescue and help me get dinner on the table in a jiffy.

Preparing healthy delicious meals in a flash is also far easier than you think. Many of these recipes meet the guidelines to healthy eating with no more that 30 per cent of calories coming from fat. What's more, many of these dishes can be prepared in a third of the time it takes to prepare them conventionally.

Not only will you come to rely on this pleasing collection of quick, easy and convenient recipes, you will start to look at your microwave in a new way — it will become your best friend in the kitchen.

— Johanna Burkhard

All About Your Microwave

How Microwave Ovens Operate

"Microwaves" are a type of energy called electromagnetic energy that travel in waves similar to radio and light waves. Microwaves are absorbed by the water, sugar and fat in food, which causes the molecules to vibrate rapidly and produce friction. The resulting heat causes the food to cook.

Microwaves are generated by a magnetron tube and sent along a waveguide into the oven cavity, which is made of metal. The waves reflect off the metal walls and floor of the oven in the same way that a mirror reflects light. Microwaves pass straight through glass, paper and most plastics to penetrate the outer edges of foods 1 to $1\frac{1}{2}$ inches (2.5 to 4 cm) in depth. The transfer of heat to the center then cooks the food in the same way as in a conventional oven. (Microwaves do not stay in food since they give up their energy as heat.)

Standing time simply allows the heat transfer to complete the cooking. Because the food absorbs the energy, the oven does not get hot and the air inside stays cool. And just as when you turn off your radio and the music stops, when you stop your microwave or open the door, the microwave energy shuts off.

What is the main difference between a microwave and a regular oven?
A microwave oven steams rather than roasts foods. It's a bit of a misnomer to refer to a microwave as an "oven" since food cooked in it rarely gets over 212°F (100°C) — the temperature that turns water to steam. A conventional oven steams foods, too, but as it can easily heat up to 400°F (200°C) or higher, roasting and toasting also go on at these much higher temperatures.

Microwave Oven Features

If you're not using your microwave to its full potential, it may be a good idea to review the instruction manual and the basic operating principles.

Today's microwave ovens are sophisticated pieces of equipment with built-in computer components and, like other appliances, require the user to be familiar with all of the features to fully maximize its cooking abilities.

If you're looking to replace your existing model, you'll find a wide range of new and improved models to choose from. One of the latest trends in the market is a selection of inexpensive ovens available with limited features, designed primarily for defrosting and reheating foods. While their inexpensive price tag may be tempting, some of these models may not be as functional when it comes to cooking with them.

Another consideration when shopping for a microwave is to make sure that your casseroles and bowls fit the compact ovens before purchasing; otherwise, you may have the added expense of buying additional dishes.

Many of the new compact microwave ovens on the market today are high-powered, with 1,000 to 1,200 watts of energy. Manufacturers, too, have streamlined the features, making them very easy to operate. Preprogrammed options — to cook popcorn and bake potatoes, for example — can be useful if they suit your cooking style.

The most useful option to look for is the sensor cook feature that automatically determines when foods are cooked or reheated. This is a real timesaver for cooks and eliminates the guesswork of weighing or measuring foods and programming cooking times.

Also helpful is the multi-stage cooking feature, whereby you can program your oven to cook at different power levels for specified times in sequence. It is terrific when cooking casseroles, rice and grain dishes, and stews.

Recently, a new line of second-generation microwaves was launched, featuring Inverter® system technology, which replaces the transformer used to transfer energy to the magnetron. Inverter® system technology uses a circuit board that allows much more flexibility and range in cooking levels, resulting in more even cooking and reheating. When the Medium (50%) power setting is used, the power is reduced to half. In traditional ovens, the power always operates on High and cycles on and off at lower power levels. It's a lot like turning a light on and off, whereas an Inverter® acts like a dimmer switch, providing a constant, even supply of power.

Another benefit of an Inverter® is that microwave ovens are much more lightweight. An Inverter® circuit board weighs 1 pound (500 g), as opposed to 10 pounds (5 kg) for a traditional microwave transformer, making microwaves less cumbersome and easier to transport.

Microwave Cooking Times

Microwave design, wattage and performance, as well as temperature and the shape of food and container used, all influence the time it takes to cook foods.

One of the biggest factors affecting cooking times in microwave recipes is the output power or wattage of an oven. It's important to know the wattage of your oven, which is usually given on the back of the microwave door or in the owner's manual. However, cooking times can vary between different brands and models, so these cooking times in recipes should be used only as a guideline.

Recipes in the *125 Best Microwave Oven Recipes* cookbook were tested in several makes and models of ovens, including the latest 1,200-watt oven and older models in the 800- to 900-watt range. The latter are not as powerful, nor do they cook as evenly as the new ovens.

All recipes include a range of cooking times to account for the variances in ovens used in today's kitchens. Because of microwave's incredible speed, it can take as little as 30 seconds to overcook certain dishes. Fast ovens should cook food in the shortest amount of time given in a recipe, while older ovens (microwaves also loose their efficiency as they age) or those with less wattage will require the longer times. As a general rule, cook foods for the shortest cooking times given and check; if not cooked enough, add extra time.

Several recipes suggest using a slightly lower power setting when using new ovens (1,200-watt range) to cook delicate foods, such as fish and eggs, while a higher power is recommended for older models (800 to 900 watts) to account for the difference in cooking quality.

What's important to remember is to use cooking times in recipes as a guideline only and to make sure you write down the new adjusted times in your recipes, so it will be easier to make the dish a second time.

Power Levels

High	100%
Medium-High	70%
Medium	50%
Medium-Low or Defrost	30%
Low	10%

Factors Affecting Cooking Time

Type of Food

Different foods absorb microwave energy at different rates and at different speeds. Microwaves are attracted to fat and sugar and heat up foods more quickly. A good example is bacon that cooks quickly and even browns.

Salt also attracts microwaves and can cause surfaces of meats and poultry to toughen when cooking. It is recommended to salt only after cooking or add salt to the liquid ingredients of the recipe to dissolve when microwaving.

Amounts

The more food in the oven, the longer it will take to microwave. If doubling a recipe or the amount of food to be cooked, such as vegetables, increase time by one-half and add on extra time as required.

Reducing Recipe Size

Most of the recipes in *125 Best Microwave Oven Recipes* serve four. To reduce the recipe size, simply divide the amount of ingredients in half. Start to microwave for half of the time stated in the recipe and increase as needed.

Generally, microwave cooking times will be approximately two-thirds of the time in the original recipe, but can vary depending on amount and type of food cooked.

Size, Shape and Density
- Uniform-cut pieces will cook more evenly than irregularly cut ones.
- Thin pieces cook faster than thick pieces. Fold under thin tapered edges (for example, fish fillets) to promote even cooking.
- Smaller pieces will cook faster than one whole piece. For example, sliced or cubed potatoes cook more quickly than a whole potato.
- Dense foods will take longer to cook.

Temperature
As with conventional cooking, cold foods from the refrigerator or frozen foods take longer to cook and reheat than if at room temperature, so adjust microwave cooking times accordingly.

Microwave Techniques

Arranging
Position thicker portions to the outer edge of the dish, with thinner portions toward the center to take into account that microwaves penetrate the outer edge of food first. Spread out foods in a single layer and space them evenly in a circle, to promote even cooking.

Stirring
Stir foods once or twice during cooking to redistribute the heat and promote even cooking. For dishes that cannot be stirred, rotate dish or turn foods over instead. (A turntable helps minimize the need, but this depends on how your oven operates.)

Piercing
Some foods come with their own natural wrapping. Pierce the skins of vegetables, such as potatoes and squash, in several places with a fork or tip of a sharp knife to allow steam to escape, so skins don't burst during cooking. Use a toothpick to pierce egg yolks in several places to prevent steam from building up and causing the yolks to explode.

Covering Foods
When cooking or reheating, cover foods with a lid, vented plastic wrap or an inverted plate to allow faster and more even cooking and reheating.

Leave foods uncovered when you want liquids to evaporate or thicken (sauces, for example). You can also loosely cover foods (such as bacon) with waxed or parchment paper or a sheet of paper towel to prevent food splatters.

Standing Time
Stir food after cooking, if possible, and let stand for a while to allow heat to distribute evenly. Carry-over heat actually continues the cooking process and raises temperatures by several degrees. Standing time will depend on type, density and volume of food.

To Clean Oven
Use a wet cloth with a mild detergent or a cleaner specifically for microwaves to periodically wipe the interior walls of oven.

To Remove Food Odors
In a large glass measure, combine 1 cup (250 mL) water with half a sliced lemon. Microwave on High for 4 to 6 minutes, then wipe surfaces with a cloth.

Defrosting and Reheating Foods in Your Microwave

Defrosting Foods in Your Microwave
The microwave is a safe and efficient way to defrost foods quickly.

- Consult your oven manual for recommended defrosting times and power levels.
- Remove food from storage wrap before thawing or heating unless the manufacturer has indicated that it is meant for microwave oven use. Place foods in a microwave-safe dish.
- For manual defrosting, use Medium-Low/Defrost (30%).
- Separate foods and remove portions as they defrost. (Drain any liquids.)
- For ground meats, once it starts to defrost, pull away defrosted portions around the edges before meat starts to cook.
- Several times during micro-defrosting, turn and rearrange food and rotate the dish.
- For foods that can be stirred, stir often.
- Foods may still have ice crystals in them when defrosted. Allow them to stand at room temperature to complete defrosting.
- Areas of food can become warm as they defrost in the microwave, so cook the food immediately.

Reheating Foods

- Store leftovers in a microwave-safe container for convenient reheating.
- Always cover foods with a lid, microwave-safe plate, vented plastic wrap (provided it does not touch the food) or parchment or waxed paper to create steam and to promote even heating. This is especially important when using the sensor reheat feature of your microwave.
- For casseroles that can be stirred or when reheating soups, liquids and foods in sauces or gravy, stir or rearrange foods often to promote even heating.
- Pasta, rice, grains and cereals reheat well on High. It may be necessary to add a small amount of water or stock — from 1 to 2 tbsp (15 to 25 mL) — for added moisture to create steam when reheating,
- Protein foods, such as chicken, meat including sliced roast beef, meat loaf, and eggs, benefit from being reheated on lower settings — Medium (50%) (new ovens) or Medium-High (70%) (older or lower-wattage ovens) — to prevent toughening. Add a small amount of stock or sauce to chicken and meat to help create steam and promote even heating.
- Vegetables overcook easily, so reheat on Medium (50%) or Medium-High (70%), stirring occasionally.
- Allow reheated foods to stand briefly before serving. Foods can appear cooler on the surface than they are inside and can cause mouth burns.
- Reheated foods should reach a steaming temperature (160°F/70°C) before serving.
- Food should steam throughout, not just around the edges. The center bottom of the plate or utensil containing the food should be very hot to the touch.

Safe Items to Use in the Microwave Oven to Cover and Wrap Foods

Plastic wrap, preferably heavy-duty plastic wrap (consult package information)
Waxed paper
Parchment paper
White paper towels and napkins
Wood and natural materials, such as wicker baskets, wooden spoons, wooden skewers and toothpicks, for short periods

NEVER USE:
Brown grocery bags
Newspaper
Metal dishes

Aluminum foil: Although generally not recommended for use in the microwave, small amounts of aluminum foil (1-inch/2.5 cm strips, not sheets) can be placed over certain areas of food, such as bones, to shield when defrosting meats. Aluminum reflects microwaves, preventing foods from overcooking. It should not touch oven walls or door.

Microwave Equipment

Microwave cooking doesn't require specialized cooking equipment other than a varied selection of good-quality heat-resistant glass-ceramic cookware (such as CorningWare), including casseroles, baking dishes, heat-tempered glass measures and bowls, which many of us already have in our kitchens. Here is a checklist of equipment called for in the *125 Best Microwave Oven Recipes* cookbook.

Casserole Dishes
- 8-cup (2 L) casserole dish with lids: have on hand two of this size of casserole dish with lids to microwave most of the recipes in this book, from rice, grains and vegetables to one-dish meals and stews.
- 4-cup (1 L) casserole dish: great for smaller amounts of vegetables and sauces.
- 12-cup (3 L) casserole dish: for larger batches of soups and stews, provided your oven is large enough to hold the dish.

Glass Measures
- 8-cup (2 L)
- 4-cup (1 L)
- 2-cup (500 mL)
- 1-cup (250 mL)

Baking Dishes
- 8-inch (2 L) square baking dish
- 11-by 7-inch (2 L) baking dish
- 10-cup (2.5 L) shallow rectangular baking dish
- 13-by 9-inch (3 L) baking dish (if it fits your oven)

Pie Plates (microwave-oven safe)
- 9-inch (23 cm) deep pie plate: two are recommended

Heat-Tempered Glass Bowls
- 4-cup (1 L) bowl
- 2-cup (500 mL) bowl
- Custard cups or ramekins

Specialized Equipment
- Bacon rack or tray
- 8-cup (2 L) ring mold for vegetables, steamed pudding and cakes
- An instant-read thermometer is recommended to check the temperature of meats and poultry. It can be used in both microwave and conventional cooking.

Melamine cookware and non-heat-resistant glass dishes are not recommended for use in microwave ovens. For ceramics, pottery and earthenware dishes: if they do not indicate that they are microwave-oven safe, it is recommended that they be tested first.

A simple test to check if a dish or container (not plastic) is microwave-oven safe: Place the empty dish in the microwave along with a 1-cup (250 mL) glass measure filled with cool water. Microwave on High for 1 minute. If microwave-oven safe, the dish will remain comfortably cool while the water will be hot. If the dish feels warm to the touch, it has absorbed microwave energy and should not be used.

Use of Plastics in the Microwave

Plastic products are handy tools to use in microwave cooking. Here's how to use them correctly.

Plastic Wrap
- Use only plastic wrap and plastic cooking bags that have been designed for the microwave. Consult the package for correct usage.
- Do not let plastic wrap touch the food. When plastic wrap comes in contact with foods heated in a microwave oven, especially those high in fat and sugar, the temperatures may be high enough to cause the plastic to melt.
- For optimal results, use a container large enough to allow 1 inch (2.5 cm) between the wrap and the food.
- When covering foods with plastic wrap, be sure to turn back one corner of the wrap to vent steam.
- As a safety precaution after cooking, remove cover away from you, to avoid steam burns.
- An alternative to plastic wrap is to use glass or ceramic lids or plates to cover dishes. Department stores now sell glass casserole lids separately; they are ideal to cover a wide variety of dishes and plates when cooking and reheating foods.

Plastic Containers

- Most cold-food packages, such as margarine tubs, yogurt and cottage cheese containers as well as foam meat trays, including foam plates and cups, are not intended for microwave use.
- Use plastic containers and dinnerware only if labeled "Microwave Oven Safe." They are designed to withstand higher temperatures but should be used only to reheat or warm foods. Excessive heating may cause the plastic to soften or even melt. Be careful to prevent spills when removing containers from the oven.
- If you can't find any labeling on a plastic container, assume it's unsafe to use in the microwave.

Adapting Recipes to the Microwave

Some recipes can be adapted to the microwave with few changes, but most recipes need adjusting as to the amount of ingredients and cooking methods. The best suggestion is to take an existing microwave recipe that is similar to the one you want to adapt to your microwave and try it.

Microwave Oven Use and Safety Tips

- Follow manufacturer's instructions concerning installation.
- Never run the microwave oven when it is empty.
- Never operate the microwave when the oven door is damaged, warped or bent.
- Never put anything but food in the microwave.
- Never pop popcorn in a brown paper bag as the bag could ignite.
- Never deep-fry in the microwave oven.
- If a flare-up or fire occurs, keep the door closed and unplug the oven or turn off circuit breaker.
- Use only microwave-safe dishes.
- Do not use metal dishes and utensils, as well as metal-trimmed plates, as they may cause arcing and damage your oven.
- Use plastic wrap correctly, as well as wrap and cover foods using paper towels, parchment and waxed paper to prevent splatters and to absorb moisture.
- Foods cooked in the microwave oven can get very hot. Have oven mitts or pot holders handy.
- Watch out for hot steam from covered dishes. Always lift lids or covers away from you.
- To prevent burns, always test foods before biting into them.

Food Safety Tips

- Ensure that the food you're cooking and reheating has been handled and stored properly.
- Refrigerate raw fish, poultry and ground meats no longer than two days before cooking or freezing. Larger cuts of meat can be refrigerated for four days, about the same length of time as for cooked foods.
- Test for Doneness for Meats and Poultry when cooking: Make sure meat and poultry have reached the recommended internal temperature throughout. Red meats should be cooked to an internal temperature of 160°F (70°C), poultry to 180°F (85°C). Use an instant-read thermometer and insert it in several places, or use the oven's temperature probe to verify if food has reached a safe temperature. For smaller pieces, cut with a knife to make sure meat is no longer pink inside and juices run clear. Where there are bones, meat should easily come away from them.
- Refrigerate leftovers shortly after cooking.
- If foods are left out for more than two hours, they should be discarded.
- Use refrigerated leftovers within three to four days.
- If you are in doubt about the safety of the food it is always best to throw it out.
- Designate a plastic cutting board to use just for meats and poultry.
- Wash work surfaces, cutting boards and utensils in hot soapy water and dry thoroughly. Periodically sanitize work surfaces and cutting boards with a small amount of bleach or disinfectant.

Appetizers and Dips

Caponata

Makes 2 cups (500 mL)

Rather than fry eggplant in oil, try this low-cal creative way to steam-cook eggplant in the microwave oven. This robust vegetable salad can be served as an appetizer or used as a condiment in hearty hero sandwiches and wraps. It's also delicious served as a topping for fish or chicken.

Tip

Filling can be refrigerated in a covered container for up to 3 days or frozen for up to 1 month.

8-cup (2 L) casserole dish with lid

2 tbsp	olive oil	25 mL
1	onion, finely chopped	1
1	large clove garlic, minced	1
4 cups	peeled eggplant, cut into $\frac{1}{2}$-inch (1 cm) cubes (about $\frac{1}{2}$ medium eggplant)	1 L
1	red bell pepper, finely diced	1
2 tbsp	tomato paste	25 mL
1	large ripe tomato, seeded and diced	1
$\frac{1}{3}$ cup	chopped black olives, such as Kalamata	75 mL
$\frac{1}{4}$ cup	chopped fresh parsley	50 mL
2 tbsp	capers, rinsed (optional)	25 mL
1 tbsp	balsamic vinegar	15 mL
	Salt and freshly ground black pepper	

1. In casserole dish, combine oil, onion, garlic, eggplant, red pepper and tomato paste. Microwave, covered, on High for 6 to 9 minutes, stirring once, until vegetables are just tender. (Eggplant should retain its shape.)

2. Stir in tomato, olives, parsley, capers, if using, and balsamic vinegar. Season with salt and pepper to taste. Let cool. Refrigerate for 2 hours or until chilled. Serve with pita crisps or crackers.

Micro-Tip

For a quick appetizer, spoon caponata into mini pitas and top with shredded Monterey Jack or mozzarella cheese. Microwave on a paper towel–lined plate on Medium (50%) for 2 to 3 minutes for 8 mini-stuffed pitas or just until cheese melts and filling is warm.

Honey Mustard Brie with Walnuts

Serves 4 to 6

Here's a quick, easy idea to dress up a small wheel of Brie. Set it out for your guests to enjoy and you won't end up spending time in the kitchen preparing fiddly hors d'oeuvres.

Tip

Toss apple and pear slices in 1 tbsp (15 mL) lemon juice to prevent discoloring.

1	wheel (7 or 8 oz/200 or 225 g) Brie or Camembert	1
1½ tbsp	honey Dijon mustard	22 mL
¼ cup	finely chopped walnuts or pecans	50 mL
	Apple and pear slices	
	Crackers	

1. With spatula, spread sides of cheese with some of the mustard and roll in chopped nuts to coat sides. Spread remaining mustard on top and sprinkle with remaining nuts.

2. Arrange nut-coated cheese on a microwave-safe serving dish. Microwave on Medium-Low (30%) for 1½ to 2½ minutes or until cheese is warm and softened.

3. Surround with apple and pear slices and crackers. Serve immediately.

Micro-Tip

Use your microwave oven to take the chill off refrigerated cheese when serving a selection of cheeses with wine or as an appetizer.

Arrange cheese on a plate and microwave on Medium-Low (30%), checking every 15 seconds until just slightly warm (watch carefully so cheese doesn't melt). Time will depend on amount and type of cheese. Let stand for 5 minutes before serving.

Spicy Thai Shrimp Wrapped in Snow Peas

Shrimp with red cocktail sauce is overdone on the party circuit. Try this spicy way to serve shrimp instead. Wrap the shrimp in snow peas, if you wish, or set out the bowl of marinated shrimp and let guests help themselves.

8-cup (2 L) casserole dish with lid

1 lb	large cooked frozen shrimp, peeled with tails left on (about 30)	500 g
2 tbsp	freshly squeezed lime juice	25 mL
2 tbsp	Thai fish sauce or soy sauce	25 mL
2 tsp	packed brown sugar	10 mL
1	large clove garlic, minced	1
1/2 tsp	Asian chili paste or to taste	2 mL
2 tbsp	chopped fresh cilantro	25 mL
30	snow peas, ends trimmed	30
	Additional cilantro for garnish	

1. Place frozen shrimp in casserole dish. Microwave, covered, on Medium (50%) for 3 to 5 minutes, stirring twice, until almost defrosted. Let stand until completely defrosted. Drain well and pat dry with paper towels. Place shrimp in a bowl.

2. In small glass measure, combine lime juice, fish sauce, brown sugar, garlic and chili paste. Microwave, uncovered, on High for 30 to 45 seconds or until fragrant. Pour over shrimp and toss to coat. Sprinkle with cilantro. Cover and refrigerate, stirring occasionally, for at least 1 hour or for up to 4 hours.

3. Rinse snow peas in cold water and place in casserole dish. Microwave, covered, on High for 1 to 1 1/2 minutes or until bright green and pliable. Rinse under cold water to chill and drain.

4. To serve, wrap a snow pea around each shrimp, securing with a toothpick. Arrange on serving platter and garnish with additional cilantro.

Appetizer Meatballs with Plum Mustard Sauce

Makes about 36 meatballs

Store-bought frozen cooked meatballs have become one of the newest convenience foods in supermarkets. I always keep a package on hand in my freezer to make these last-minute tasty appetizers.

4-cup (1 L) casserole dish with lid

¾ cup	bottled plum sauce	175 mL
2 tbsp	soy sauce	25 mL
1 tbsp	Dijon mustard	15 mL
2 tsp	minced fresh gingerroot	10 mL
1 lb	frozen cooked meatballs (about 36)	500 g
1	green onion, sliced	1

1. In casserole dish, combine plum sauce, soy sauce, 2 tbsp (25 mL) water, mustard and ginger. Add frozen meatballs and stir to coat with sauce.

2. Microwave, covered, on High for 7 to 10 minutes, stirring twice, until piping hot and meatballs are heated through in center. Transfer to a serving dish and sprinkle with green onions. Serve immediately.

Micro-Tip

Never overload your microwave by trying to heat a large amount of frozen food at once. If you want to reheat double the amount of meatballs, for example, do it in two batches and make sure to stir often to promote even reheating.

All-Dressed Pizza Pockets

Makes 4

Here's a terrific alternative to store-bought pizza pockets that makes a fun after-school snack or light supper easy enough for young kids to make.

Bacon rack (optional)

3	slices bacon (optional)	3
1 cup	shredded mozzarella cheese	250 mL
1/2 cup	thinly sliced mushrooms (4 or 5)	125 mL
1/4 cup	sliced pepperoni, cut into strips	50 mL
1/2	green bell pepper, cut into thin 1-inch (2.5 cm) strips	1/2
2 tbsp	sliced black or green olives (optional)	25 mL
1/2 cup	pizza sauce, divided	125 mL
2	pita breads (7 inches/18 cm), halved to form pockets	2

1. Place bacon, if using, on a bacon rack or paper towel–lined plate and top with a paper towel to prevent splatters. Microwave on High for 2 to 3$\frac{1}{2}$ minutes or until crisp. Let cool and crumble.

2. In a bowl, combine bacon bits, cheese, mushrooms, pepperoni, green pepper and olives, if using.

3. Spread 2 tbsp (25 mL) of the pizza sauce in each pita pocket half. Fill with $\frac{1}{2}$ cup (125 mL) of the cheese mixture.

4. Place stuffed pita pockets on paper towel–lined plate and cover with another sheet of paper towel. Microwave on Medium-High (70%) for 2 to 3 minutes or until pitas are warm to the touch and cheese melts.

Micro-Tip

To heat one pizza pocket: Wrap in paper towel and place on plate. Microwave on Medium-High (70%) for 30 to 45 seconds.

Microwave Oven Use and Safety Tips for Kids

▪ Teach children how to use the microwave oven safely and correctly. Remember these safety rules:
1. Never run the microwave oven when it is empty.
2. Never put anything but food in the microwave.
3. Never leave the microwave oven unattended when turned on.
4. Never pop popcorn in a brown paper bag as the bag can ignite.
5. If a flare up or fire occurs, keep door closed, unplug the oven or turn off circuit breaker.

▪ Tips on reheating food:
1. Know what dishes can be used in the microwave oven. Metal dishes and utensils, as well as metal-trimmed plates, will cause arcing. Use a permanent marker to identify which glass, ceramic and plastic dishes are microwave-safe.
2. Use plastic wrap correctly as well as wrap and cover foods using paper towels, parchment and waxed paper to prevent food splatters and absorb moisture.
3. Heatproof glass bowls and measures with handles are easier to place in and out of the microwave.
4. If reheating a single serving, set plate or bowl on another larger plate to make it easier to remove dish from oven.
5. Foods cooked in the microwave oven can get very hot. Have oven mitts or pot holders handy.
6. Watch out for hot steam from covered dishes. Always lift lids or covers from dishes away from you.
7. Not sure about how long a food should be heated in the microwave oven? Start out using a short microwave time, then check food and continue to microwave if needed.
8. Always test foods before biting into to prevent burns.
9. To cut down on waste, use dishes that can be washed rather than using disposables, such as paper plates, in the microwave.

▪ **Recipe suggestions with kid appeal that they can help make and enjoy!**

All-Dressed Pizza Pockets	Maple Baked Apples
Amazing Turkey Enchiladas	Mushroom Cheese Muffin Melt
Baked Potatoes with	Peanut Butter Fudge Sauce
Broccoli Cheese Sauce	Peanut Butter Raisin Crispies
Brown Sugar Apples with Raisins	Pizza Baked Potatoes
Chicken Caesar Wrap	Quick Scrambled Eggs
Chili Sloppy Joes	Quick Vegetable Lasagna
Chocolate Pudding Cake	Raisin Nut Popcorn Balls
Creamy Rice Pudding	Rocky Road Popcorn
Creamy Salsa and Cheese Dip	So Easy Chili
Easy Baked Beans	Sweet-and-Sour Meatballs
Homespun Macaroni and Cheese	with Vegetables
Italian Beef Heroes	Tuna Mushroom Bake

Appetizer Meatballs with Spicy Chili Sauce

For meatballs with a fiery kick, add more chili paste or use your favorite hot pepper sauce to taste.

4-cup (1 L) casserole dish with lid

³⁄₄ cup	bottled chili sauce	175 mL
¹⁄₂ cup	grape jelly	125 mL
1 to 2 tsp	Asian chili paste	5 to 10 mL
1 lb	frozen cooked meatballs (about 36)	500 g

1. In casserole dish, combine chili sauce, grape jelly and Asian chili paste. Microwave, uncovered, on High for 1 to 1¹⁄₂ minutes, stirring once, until hot and jelly is melted. Add frozen meatballs and stir to coat with sauce.

2. Microwave, covered, on High for 7 to 10 minutes, stirring twice, until meatballs are piping hot and heated through in center. Transfer to serving dish and serve immediately.

Garlic and Herb Pita Toasts

Makes 32 pieces

I always have a package of pita breads on hand in the freezer to make these great-tasting last-minute appetizers. Instead of garlic bread, serve these crispy wedges to accompany soup, pasta or salad.

Variation

Try other herb and spice combinations, such as chili powder and oregano, or crumbled rosemary and finely grated lemon zest. Or omit the herbs and rely on the garlic and Parmesan for flavoring.

2 tbsp	butter	25 mL
1	clove garlic, minced	1
1/4 tsp	dried basil leaves	1 mL
1/4 tsp	dried oregano leaves	1 mL
2	white or whole wheat thin pita breads (7 inches/18 cm)	2
1/4 cup	freshly grated Parmesan cheese	50 mL

1. Place butter, garlic, basil and oregano in a small glass measure. Microwave, uncovered, on High for 30 to 45 seconds or until bubbling.

2. Split pita breads into rounds. Brush each pita half, cut side up, with garlic herb butter. Sprinkle with cheese. Cut each round into 8 wedges.

3. Place half of the wedges on a large paper towel–lined plate. Microwave, uncovered, on High for 2 to 3 minutes, rearranging wedges once, until golden. (Be careful that they don't burn.) Repeat with remaining wedges. Toasts will crisp as they cool. (Or place toasts on a baking sheet and bake in 350°F/180°C oven for 7 to 9 minutes or until golden and crisp.)

Creamy Salsa and Cheese Dip

Makes 2 cups
(500 mL)

This popular dip also makes a terrific topping for baked potatoes. Not everyone enjoys a spicy dip. Use a mild salsa and add additional jalapeño peppers or hot pepper sauce according to the preference of your guests.

4-cup (1 L) casserole dish

¾ cup	light (5%) cream or milk	175 mL
2 tbsp	butter	25 mL
1	small clove garlic, minced	1
2 tbsp	all-purpose flour	25 mL
1 cup	shredded aged Cheddar cheese	250 mL
1 cup	mild or medium salsa	250 mL
1 to 2 tbsp	chopped pickled jalapeño peppers	15 to 25 mL
	Tortilla chips or raw vegetables	

1. In a small glass measure, microwave cream, uncovered, on High for 1 to 1½ minutes or until piping hot.

2. In casserole dish, microwave butter, uncovered, and garlic on High for 30 to 45 seconds or until bubbling. Blend in flour. Whisk in hot cream until smooth. Microwave, uncovered, on High for 1½ to 2 minutes, stirring once, until sauce boils and thickens.

3. Stir in cheese until melted. Stir in salsa and jalapeño peppers. Microwave, uncovered, on High for 1 to 1½ minutes or until piping hot. Serve warm with tortilla chips or raw vegetables as dippers.

Micro-Tip

Dip can be made up to 3 days ahead. Let cool, cover and refrigerate. To serve, reheat, uncovered, on High for 1½ to 2½ minutes, stirring twice, until warm.

Red Pepper and White Bean Dip

I like to serve this tasty, easy-to-make spread with warm squares of focaccia or pita crisps, or tortilla chips.

Tip

Dip can be covered and refrigerated for up to 3 days before serving.

Variation

Red Pepper and White Bean Dip with Feta Substitute parsley for basil. Add 1 tsp (5 mL) dried oregano leaves along with red pepper and onions when cooking. Use feta cheese instead of goat cheese.

4-cup (1 L) casserole dish with lid

2 tbsp	olive oil	25 mL
1	small onion, chopped	1
2	large cloves garlic, chopped	2
1	red bell pepper, chopped	1
1 tbsp	balsamic vinegar	15 mL
¼ tsp	hot pepper flakes	1 mL
1	can (19 oz/540 mL) white kidney beans, drained and rinsed	1
4 oz	goat cheese, crumbled	125 g
2 tbsp	chopped fresh basil	25 mL

1. In casserole dish, combine oil, onion, garlic, red pepper, balsamic vinegar and hot pepper flakes. Microwave, covered, on High for 5 to 8 minutes, stirring once, until vegetables are very tender.

2. In a food processor, purée kidney beans and vegetable mixture until smooth. Add goat cheese and process just until combined.

3. Transfer to a bowl. Stir in basil. Cover and refrigerate until chilled.

Warm Salmon Dip

**Makes 1³⁄₄ cups
(425 mL)**

When it comes to assembling a quick appetizer, I count on this recipe, which serves as a base for other canned seafood such as shrimp, crab or tuna. Serve this inviting dip with an assortment of crisp raw vegetables or crackers.

Tips

Remove skins in canned salmon but mash in the soft bones for added calcium.

Sockeye salmon provides the best flavor and color.

1	package (8 oz/250 g) cream cheese, cubed	1
2 tbsp	seafood cocktail sauce	25 mL
1 tsp	freshly squeezed lemon juice	5 mL
1 tsp	Worcestershire sauce	5 mL
Dash	hot pepper sauce	Dash
1	can (7¹⁄₂ oz/213 g) salmon, juice reserved, flaked (see Tips, left)	1
2 tbsp	chopped fresh dill, chives or parsley	25 mL

1. In a microwave-safe bowl, microwave cream cheese, uncovered, on Medium (50%) for 1 to 1¹⁄₂ minutes or until softened. Stir until smooth. Blend in seafood cocktail sauce, lemon juice, Worcestershire and hot pepper sauce.

2. Flake salmon, discarding skin. Add to bowl with 2 tbsp (25 mL) reserved juice (or use milk) and dill.

3. Microwave, uncovered, on Medium (50%) for 1¹⁄₂ to 2 minutes, stirring once, until heated through. Serve warm.

Warm Mushroom Parmesan Spread

Makes 2 cups (500 mL)

■ This flavorful appetizer is one that I rely on most when planning a special dinner party, and it is the recipe most-requested by friends.

Tip

Dip can be placed in a covered container and frozen for up to 1 month.

Variation

Mushroom Crostini
To make crostini: Cut 1 baguette into 1/3-inch (8 mm) thick slices. Arrange on baking sheet. Brush lightly with olive oil. Bake in 375°F (190°C) oven for 5 minutes or until edges are lightly toasted. Spread toasts with mushroom mixture just before baking to prevent them from turning soggy. Arrange on baking sheet. Sprinkle with additional Parmesan cheese. Bake in 375°F (190°C) oven for 7 to 8 minutes or until heated through.

8-cup (2 L) glass measure

2 tbsp	butter	25 mL
4 cups	finely chopped cremini mushrooms (about 12 oz/375 g)	1 L
1/4 cup	finely chopped shallots	50 mL
2	cloves garlic, minced	2
1 1/2 tsp	chopped fresh thyme or 1/2 tsp (2 mL) dried thyme leaves	7 mL
1 tbsp	all-purpose flour	15 mL
1/2 cup	whipping (35%) cream	125 mL
2 tbsp	medium-dry sherry or rye whisky	25 mL
1/2 tsp	salt	2 mL
	Freshly ground black pepper	
1/4 cup	freshly grated Parmesan cheese	50 mL
2 tbsp	finely chopped fresh parsley	25 mL

1. In glass measure, combine butter, mushrooms, shallots, garlic and thyme. Microwave, uncovered, on High for 5 to 8 minutes, stirring once, until mushrooms are tender.

2. Stir in flour until blended. Stir in cream, sherry, salt, and pepper to taste. Microwave, uncovered, on High for 4 to 6 minutes, stirring once, until thickened. Stir in Parmesan and parsley.

3. To serve, spoon into serving dish and surround with crackers, pita crisps or crostini.

Micro-Tip

■ If making ahead, cover and refrigerate for up to 2 days. Reheat on High for 1 1/2 to 2 minutes, stirring once, until piping hot.

Salsa Crab Spread

Makes 2 cups (500 mL)

Simple, easy and always a hit. Serve with crackers or tortilla chips.

Tip

Be sure to remove any shell and cartilage from canned crabmeat.

1	package (8 oz/250 g) cream cheese, cubed	1
1	can (6 oz/170 g) crabmeat, drained (see Tip, left)	1
1/2 cup	well-drained mild or medium chunky salsa	125 mL
2 tbsp	chopped fresh cilantro (optional)	25 mL

1. In a microwave-safe bowl, microwave cream cheese, uncovered, on Medium (50%) for 1 to $1\frac{1}{2}$ minutes or until softened. Stir until smooth. Blend in crabmeat and salsa.

2. Microwave, uncovered, on Medium (50%) for $1\frac{1}{2}$ to 2 minutes, stirring once, until heated through. Stir in cilantro, if using. Serve warm with crackers.

Micro-Tip

To recrisp cereal or snack foods such as potato chips, crackers, pretzels, tortilla and nacho chips, arrange about 2 cups (500 mL) in a single layer on a paper towel–lined plate or wicker basket. Microwave on High for 30 to 60 seconds, tossing once, until warm. Time depends on amount and type of snack food or cereal. Watch carefully to prevent scorching.

Soups and Chowders

Asian Chicken Noodle Soup

Healthy old-fashioned chicken soup gets an Asian spin here with rice vermicelli noodles, snow peas and other goodies. Hearty steaming bowls of this soup are reminiscent of the Vietnamese pho soups that have become popular in restaurants.

Tip

I find the best flavor comes from using fresh chicken breasts, but 1$\frac{1}{2}$ cups (375 mL) leftover cooked chicken or turkey can be substituted. Instead of rice vermicelli, use the noodles from 1 package (3 oz/85 g) instant ramen noodles (omit the packaged seasoning mix that comes with it).

8-cup (2 L) casserole dish with lid or glass measure covered with vented plastic wrap

4 cups	chicken stock	1 L
2 tsp	minced fresh gingerroot	10 mL
1 cup	broken rice vermicelli	250 mL
1	large carrot, peeled and grated	1
2	small skinless boneless chicken breasts (8 oz/250 g)	2
1$\frac{1}{2}$ cups	snow peas, ends trimmed, cut on the diagonal into 3 pieces each	375 mL
1$\frac{1}{2}$ cups	bean sprouts	375 mL
1	large green onion, sliced	1
1 tsp	sesame oil	5 mL
	Soy sauce and Asian chili oil for seasoning	

1. In casserole dish, combine stock and ginger. Cover with a plate or plastic wrap with one corner turned back to vent. Microwave on High for 6 to 9 minutes or until boiling. Add noodles and carrot. Microwave, covered, for 4 to 6 minutes or until noodles are softened.

2. Cut chicken into very thin strips. Add to stock along with snow peas. Microwave, covered, on High for 2 to 4 minutes or until chicken is no longer pink and snow peas are tender-crisp.

3. Stir in bean sprouts, green onions and sesame oil. Let stand, covered, for 2 minutes. Ladle into bowls and season with soy sauce and Asian chili oil to taste.

Honey Mustard Brie with Walnuts (page 19)

Chilled Corn and Red Pepper Soup

Serves 4

This colorful soup has no added fat, so indulge in a second bowl without guilt.

Tips

To cut corn kernels from cobs, stand ears on end and cut straight down using a small sharp knife.

Fresh corn, which is now readily available year-round, is preferred in this recipe. You can use frozen corn in a pinch, but the taste may not be as sweet so add an extra pinch of sugar to taste, if needed.

8-cup (2 L) casserole dish with lid or glass measure covered with vented plastic wrap

2	red bell peppers, chopped	2
4	green onions, sliced	4
1	large clove garlic, chopped	1
2 cups	chicken stock	500 mL
1½ cups	fresh corn kernels (2 to 3 cobs) or frozen corn (see Tips, left)	375 mL
1 cup	plain nonfat yogurt	250 mL
Pinch	granulated sugar	Pinch
	Salt and freshly ground black pepper	
	Hot pepper sauce	
2 tbsp	chopped fresh cilantro, chives or parsley	25 mL

1. In casserole dish, combine red peppers, green onions, garlic and stock. Microwave, covered, on High for 8 to 12 minutes or until peppers are tender when pierced with a fork.

2. Add corn. Microwave, covered, on High for 4 to 7 minutes or until corn is tender. Let cool slightly.

3. In a food processor or blender, purée in batches until smooth. Strain soup through a fine sieve to remove pepper skins. Whisk in yogurt. Add sugar. Stir in salt, pepper and hot pepper sauce to taste.

4. Cover and refrigerate for about 4 hours or until chilled, or overnight. To serve, ladle into chilled bowls and sprinkle with chopped cilantro.

Chilled Corn and
Red Pepper Soup (this page)

Chilled Zucchini Soup with Cilantro

Serves 4

Here's a fast soup that makes use of both your food processor and microwave, requiring hardly any time to make.

Tip

When there is an abundance of fresh garden zucchini, make extra batches of this soup to have handy in your freezer. Omit cream and freeze in a covered storage container for up to 2 months. Place soup in an 8-cup (2 L) glass measure. Microwave on High, stirring often to break up lumps, until defrosted. Stir in cream. Refrigerate until serving time. Or, microwave until piping hot.

8-cup (2 L) casserole dish with lid or glass measure covered with vented plastic wrap

5 cups	grated zucchini (about 3)	1.25 L
1	onion, grated	1
1	large clove garlic, chopped	1
1½ tsp	mild curry paste or powder	7 mL
1	can (10 oz/284 mL) condensed chicken broth, undiluted	1
1 cup	half-and-half (10%) cream or buttermilk	250 mL
	Salt and freshly ground black pepper	
2 tbsp	chopped fresh cilantro or chives	25 mL

1. In casserole dish, combine zucchini, onion, garlic, curry paste and chicken broth. Microwave, covered, on High for 10 to 14 minutes or until zucchini is very tender. Let cool slightly.

2. In a food processor or blender, purée in batches until smooth. Return to casserole dish and stir in cream.

3. Cover and refrigerate for about 4 hours or until chilled. Season with salt and pepper to taste. To serve, ladle into chilled bowls and sprinkle with cilantro.

4. To serve hot, microwave, covered, on High for 3 to 5 minutes (5 to 8 minutes, if refrigerated), stirring twice, until piping hot. Do not let soup boil or it may curdle.

Micro-Tip

An advantage of cooking cream-based soups in the microwave is that there's no need to worry about scorching the bottom as you do on the stovetop.

Creamy Cauliflower Soup with Feta and Dill

Feta and dill are a wonderful flavor combination in this creamy soup that is great to serve when entertaining.

8-cup (2 L) casserole dish with lid or glass measure covered with vented plastic wrap

1	leek, white and light green part only, sliced	1
5 cups	small cauliflower florets (about 1 small head)	1.25 L
2 cups	chicken stock	500 mL
1 cup	diced peeled potato	250 mL
1 cup	half-and-half (10%) cream or milk	250 mL
2 tbsp	chopped fresh dill	25 mL
	Salt and freshly ground black pepper	
½ cup	crumbled feta cheese	125 mL
	Dill sprigs as garnish	

1. In casserole dish, combine leek, cauliflower, stock and potato. Microwave, covered, on High for 14 to 18 minutes or until vegetables are very tender. Let cool slightly.

2. In a food processor or blender, purée in batches until smooth. Return to casserole dish and stir in cream and dill. Season with salt and pepper to taste.

3. Microwave, covered, on High for 3 to 5 minutes, stirring once, until piping hot. Do not let soup boil or it may curdle.

4. Ladle into bowls and top each with 2 tbsp (25 mL) feta cheese. Garnish bowls with sprigs of dill.

Micro-Tip

When using an 8-cup (2 L) glass measure or casserole dish without a matching lid, cover with plastic wrap, with one corner turned back to vent. Or cover with a microwave-safe plate; it works like a charm and you won't always have to rely on plastic wrap as a cover.

Moroccan-Spiced Carrot Soup

<table>
<tr><td>**Serves 4**</td></tr>
</table>

In this exotically spiced soup, cinnamon plays a key role. Don't think of it as for desserts only. Here, it combines with cumin and coriander, and the results are sublime.

8-cup (2 L) casserole dish with lid or glass measure covered with vented plastic wrap

2 tbsp	butter	25 mL
1	leek, white and light green part only, sliced	1
1	large clove garlic, chopped	1
1 tsp	ground cumin	5 mL
1 tsp	ground coriander	5 mL
1/2 tsp	ground cinnamon	2 mL
2 cups	whole baby carrots, coarsely chopped	500 mL
1 cup	diced potato	250 mL
2 1/2 cups	chicken stock (approx.)	625 mL
1 cup	half-and-half (10%) cream	250 mL
	Salt and freshly ground black pepper	
2 tbsp	chopped fresh chives or cilantro	25 mL

1. In casserole dish, combine butter, leek, garlic, cumin, coriander and cinnamon. Microwave, covered, on High for 3 to 4 minutes, stirring once, until leek is softened.

2. Add carrots, potato and stock. Microwave, covered, on High for 15 to 20 minutes or until vegetables are very tender. Let cool slightly.

3. In a food processor or blender, purée in batches until smooth. Return to casserole dish and stir in cream. Thin with additional stock, if desired. Season with salt and pepper to taste.

4. To serve soup hot, microwave, covered, on High, for 3 to 5 minutes (5 to 8 minutes, if refrigerated), stirring once, until piping hot. Do not let soup boil or it may curdle. To serve cold, cover and refrigerate for about 4 hours, until chilled, or overnight. Ladle soup into bowls and sprinkle with chives.

Lemon Broccoli Soup

Serves 4

This refreshing soup can either be served piping hot or enjoyed chilled on a hot summer day.

8-cup (2 L) casserole dish with lid or glass measure covered with vented plastic wrap

2 tbsp	butter	25 mL
1	large onion, chopped	1
2 tbsp	all-purpose flour	25 mL
2 cups	chicken stock, divided	500 mL
4 cups	finely chopped fresh broccoli	1 L
2 cups	light (5%) cream or milk	500 mL
1 tsp	finely grated lemon zest	5 mL
	Salt and freshly ground black pepper	
2 tbsp	chopped fresh herbs such as chives, cilantro, basil or parsley	25 mL

1. In casserole dish, combine butter and onion. Microwave, covered, on High for 2 to 3 minutes or until onion is softened.

2. In a bowl, blend flour with $\frac{1}{3}$ cup (75 mL) of the stock until smooth. Stir into casserole along with remaining stock and broccoli. Microwave, covered, on High for 8 to 12 minutes, stirring once, until broccoli is tender. Let cool slightly.

3. In a food processor or blender, purée soup in batches until smooth. Return to casserole dish and stir in cream and lemon zest. Season with salt and pepper to taste.

4. To serve soup hot, microwave, covered, on High for 3 to 5 minutes (5 to 8 minutes, if refrigerated), stirring once, until piping hot. To serve cold, cover and refrigerate for about 4 hours, until chilled, or overnight. Ladle soup into bowls and sprinkle with herbs.

Mushroom Lentil Soup

Use convenient canned lentils to make this nourishing main course soup in your microwave oven. Serve with whole grain bread and a side salad to complete the meal.

Tip

To save time, chop the onions and mushrooms in the food processor, using on-off turns.

8-cup (2 L) casserole dish with lid or glass measure covered with vented plastic wrap

1 tbsp	vegetable oil	15 mL
1	onion, chopped	1
2	cloves garlic, minced	2
2 cups	chopped mushrooms (about 6 oz/175 g)	500 mL
1/2 tsp	dried thyme or marjoram leaves	2 mL
1	can (19 oz/540 mL) lentils, drained and rinsed	1
3 cups	chicken or vegetable stock (approx.)	750 mL
2 tbsp	chopped fresh dill or parsley	25 mL
	Freshly ground black pepper	

1. In casserole dish, combine oil, onion, garlic, mushrooms and thyme. Microwave, covered, on High for 5 to 8 minutes, stirring once, until vegetables are tender.

2. Add lentils and stock. Microwave, covered, on High for 8 to 12 minutes or until soup is piping hot. Stir in dill. Thin with additional stock, if needed. Season with pepper to taste.

Micro-Tips

To quickly heat a large amount of soup, cover with a lid, microwave-safe plate or vented plastic wrap, stirring often to promote even heating.

Heat leftover soup, covered, on High allowing about 1 minute per cup (250 mL) of soup. (Time will depend on type of soup. Add more time if required.)

To reheat an individual bowl of soup (1 1/2 cups/375 mL), microwave, uncovered, on High, stirring often, for 2 to 3 minutes or until piping hot.

Cheesy Italian Vegetable Chowder

Serves 4

Turn convenient frozen vegetables into a soothing main-course soup to combat winter chills. Just pair with crusty bread for a complete and satisfying dinner.

Tips

If frozen vegetables are large, chop into smaller pieces.

Cook about 1/3 cup (75 mL) extra rice or 1/2 cup (125 mL) pasta such as macaroni the night before to have on hand for this great-tasting soup.

8-cup (2 L) casserole dish with lid or glass measure covered with vented plastic wrap

1 tbsp	butter	15 mL
1	small onion, chopped	1
1	clove garlic, minced	1
1 tsp	dried basil leaves	5 mL
2 tbsp	all-purpose flour	25 mL
1 1/2 cups	chicken or vegetable stock (approx.), divided	375 mL
2 cups	frozen Italian mixed vegetables (see Tips, left)	500 mL
1 cup	milk	250 mL
1 cup	cooked rice or small pasta shapes (see Tips, left)	250 mL
1 cup	shredded Cheddar cheese	250 mL
	Salt and freshly ground black pepper	

1. In casserole dish, combine butter, onion, garlic and basil. Microwave, covered, on High for 2 to 3 minutes or until onion is softened.

2. In a bowl, blend flour with 1/3 cup (75 mL) of the stock until smooth. Stir into onion mixture along with remaining stock and frozen vegetables. Microwave, covered, on High for 8 to 12 minutes, stirring once, until vegetables are tender.

3. Stir in milk and rice. Microwave, covered, on High for 4 to 6 minutes or until piping hot.

4. Add cheese. Let stand, covered, for 2 minutes or until cheese melts. Thin soup with additional stock, if desired. Season with salt and pepper to taste.

Tomato Clam Chowder

Here's a hearty main-course soup to serve with crusty whole grain rolls and a wedge of Cheddar for an easy supper.

Variation

Tomato Fish Chowder
Instead of clams, use 8 oz (250 g) fish fillets, such as cod, bluefish or haddock, cut into $3/4$-inch (2 cm) chunks. Increase stock to 2 cups (500 mL). Add fish at the end along with parsley. Microwave on High for 2 to 3 minutes or until fish is opaque.

8-cup (2 L) casserole dish with lid or glass measure covered with vented plastic wrap

4	strips bacon, finely chopped	4
1	onion, chopped	1
1 cup	potato, peeled and diced	250 mL
2	carrots, peeled and diced	2
$1/2$ tsp	dried thyme leaves	2 mL
1	can (5 oz/140 g) clams, including juice	1
1	can (19 oz/540 mL) stewed tomatoes, chopped, including juice	1
$1^1/_2$ cups	chicken stock	375 mL
2 tbsp	chopped fresh parsley	25 mL
	Freshly ground black pepper	

1. In casserole dish, sprinkle bacon in a single layer. Microwave on High for 3 to 5 minutes or until crisp. Remove and place on paper towels to drain. Drain off all but 1 tbsp (15 mL) of drippings from dish.

2. Add onion, potato, carrot and thyme to casserole dish. Microwave, covered, on High for 5 to 8 minutes, stirring once, until vegetables are tender.

3. Add clams with juice, stewed tomatoes with juice and stock. Microwave, covered, on High for 10 to 14 minutes, stirring once, until boiling and flavors blend.

4. Add bacon bits and parsley. Season with pepper to taste.

Salmon and Dill Chowder

This hearty chowder offers a boost of calcium. Remove skin in canned salmon but crush and add the calcium-rich bones along with liquid for extra flavor.

Tip

If fresh dill is unavailable, use 1 tsp (5 mL) dried dillweed instead. Add along with onion mixture.

8-cup (2 L) casserole dish with lid or glass measure covered with vented plastic wrap

1 tbsp	butter	15 mL
1	small onion, finely chopped	1
2	carrots, peeled and finely diced	2
1½ cups	finely diced potatoes (about 2)	375 mL
3 tbsp	all-purpose flour	45 mL
1½ cups	chicken stock, divided	375 mL
1 cup	milk	250 mL
1	can (7½ oz/213 g) salmon, including juice and bones	1
2 tbsp	chopped fresh dill (see Tip, left)	25 mL
	Salt and freshly ground black pepper	

1. In casserole dish, combine butter, onion, carrots and potatoes. Microwave, covered, on High for 7 to 10 minutes, stirring once, until vegetables are tender.

2. In a bowl, blend flour with $\frac{1}{3}$ cup (75 mL) of the stock until smooth. Add to vegetable mixture along with remaining stock. Microwave, covered, on High for 3 to 5 minutes, stirring once, until thickened.

3. Stir in milk, salmon with juice and bones, and salt and pepper to taste. Microwave, covered, on High for 3 to 5 minutes or until piping hot.

Bean and Pasta Chowder with Basil Pesto

Even if the fridge is almost bare, you can rustle up a nourishing meal with a few pantry staples. If you like, add diced smoked ham for the last few minutes of cooking time and heat through.

Tips

To easily chop the canned tomatoes, leave in can and run a knife through the tomatoes.

Canned beans and legumes such as lentils are quite salty, so drain in a sieve or colander and give a quick rinse under cold water to get rid of the excess salt.

8-cup (2 L) casserole dish with lid or glass measure covered with vented plastic wrap

2 cups	chicken stock	500 mL
½ cup	dried pasta, such as small shells	125 mL
1	can (19 oz/540 mL) white kidney beans, drained and rinsed, divided (see Tips, left)	1
1	can (19 oz/540 mL) Italian-style stewed tomatoes, chopped, including juice (see Tips, left)	1
2 tbsp	basil pesto sauce or to taste	25 mL
	Freshly ground black pepper	
	Freshly grated Parmesan cheese	

1. In casserole dish, combine chicken stock and pasta. Microwave, covered, on High for 6 to 9 minutes, stirring once, until pasta is almost tender.

2. In a bowl, mash half of the beans using a fork. Add mashed beans, remaining whole beans and stewed tomatoes with juice to casserole dish. Microwave, covered, on High for 8 to 12 minutes, stirring once, until piping hot. Stir in pesto and season with pepper to taste.

3. Ladle into bowls and sprinkle with Parmesan cheese.

Breakfast and Brunch

Creamy Scrambled Eggs with Ham

You'll love the way eggs turn out in the microwave — so light and creamy. Serve with toasted bagels for a special weekend breakfast or brunch.

Tip

Lower-wattage ovens are 900 watts and under. Higher-wattage ovens are 1,000 and more. For more information on oven powers, see page 9.

Variation

Creamy Scrambled Eggs with Smoked Salmon Instead of ham, add ½ cup (125 mL) thin strips smoked salmon. When eggs are set, sprinkle with 1 tbsp (15 mL) chopped fresh dill.

8-cup (2 L) casserole dish or glass measure

1 tbsp	butter	15 mL
3	green onions, sliced	3
2 oz	cream cheese, cubed (¼ cup/50 mL)	60 g
8	eggs	8
¼ cup	milk	50 mL
½ cup	finely chopped smoked ham	125 mL
	Salt and freshly ground black pepper	

1. In a microwave-safe bowl, combine butter and green onions. Microwave, uncovered, on High for 1 to 1½ minutes or until softened. Add cream cheese. Microwave, uncovered, on High for 30 to 45 seconds or until softened. Whisk until smooth.

2. Break eggs into casserole dish. Whisk in cream cheese mixture and milk until smooth. Stir in ham and season with salt and pepper.

3. Microwave, uncovered, on Medium (50%) for new ovens and Medium-High (70%) for older or lower-wattage ovens for 5 to 7 minutes, stirring every 1½ minutes, until eggs are almost set but still a bit moist. (Undercook slightly as eggs continue to set upon standing.) Let stand, covered, for 2 minutes.

Quick Scrambled Eggs

This easy starter is ready in about the same time as it takes to make toast. The recipe can be varied according to what you have on hand. For a simple lunch or dinner, add a pinch of dried herbs or fresh chopped herbs, such as parsley, and one small diced seeded tomato. Of course, it's great for breakfast, too!

Variation

Egg Salsa Wrap
Wrap 2 small (7 inches/18 cm) flour tortillas in paper towels and microwave on High for 30 to 60 seconds or until warm. Spoon warm scrambled eggs along bottom third of each tortilla. Top each with 1 tbsp (15 mL) salsa. Fold 1 inch (2.5 cm) of the right and left sides of tortilla over filling. Starting from bottom, roll up tortilla and serve.

2	eggs	2
2 tbsp	milk or water	25 mL
2 tbsp	shredded Cheddar cheese (optional)	25 mL
2 tbsp	finely chopped ham or bacon bits (optional)	25 mL
	Salt and freshly ground black pepper	

1. Crack eggs into microwave-safe cereal bowl. Add milk, cheese and/or ham, if using. Season with salt and pepper. Beat lightly with a fork.

2. Microwave, uncovered, on Medium (50%) for new ovens and Medium-High (70%) for older or lower-wattage ovens for 1 minute 15 seconds to $2^1/_2$ minutes, stirring twice, until eggs are creamy and almost set. (Undercook slightly as eggs continue to set upon standing.)

Micro-Tips

Microwaving Eggs
Eggs and the microwave make a good team, producing excellent results with a minimum of cleanup. Here are a few tips to keep in mind when microwaving eggs.

• Microwave times in recipes are based on large eggs at refrigerator temperature. Adjust times accordingly if using different-size eggs.
• Never cook an egg in the shell as it will explode and make a mess in your oven.
• For fluffy scrambled eggs, add additional moisture (1 tbsp/15 mL water or milk per egg). When scrambling eggs, use Medium (50%) for new ovens and Medium-High (70%) for older or lower-wattage ovens.
• When cooking an unbeaten egg (out of the shell), always use a toothpick or tip of a sharp knife to pierce the egg yolk in several places to prevent steam from building up and causing the yolk to explode. Also, use a lower power setting, such as Medium-Low (30%) for new ovens or Medium (50%) for older or lower-wattage ovens, as the fat content in an egg yolk causes it to cook more quickly than the white.
• When making an airy soufflé or a puffy omelet, use your regular oven. Results are less than satisfactory in the microwave for these egg preparations.

Egg Tomato Muffin Melt with Bacon

No time to make breakfast? For a portable breakfast on the run, make these muffin melts the day before and reheat briefly.

Bacon rack (optional)
Two 6-oz (175 mL) custard cups or ramekins, buttered

2	slices bacon, halved	2
2	eggs	2
2	English muffins, split, toasted and buttered, if desired	2
4	thin slices tomato	4
	Salt and freshly ground black pepper	
1/4 cup	shredded aged Cheddar cheese	50 mL

1. Place bacon on a bacon rack or paper towel–lined plate. Cover with a paper towel. Microwave on High for 1 1/2 to 3 minutes or until crisp. Set aside.

2. Break an egg into each custard cup. Using a toothpick, pierce each yolk gently 3 to 4 times. Cover dishes with plastic wrap and turn back one corner to vent.

3. Microwave on Medium-Low (30%) for 2 to 3 minutes or until egg whites are just set and yolks are still runny. For older or lower-wattage ovens, increase to Medium (50%) and cook eggs for 2 1/2 to 4 minutes, rearranging dish once during cooking.

4. Place 2 muffin halves on a paper towel–lined plate. Top with 2 half slices bacon and 2 tomato slices. Remove eggs from cups and place on top of tomatoes. Season with salt and pepper to taste. Sprinkle with cheese.

5. Microwave, uncovered, on Medium (50%) for 1 to 2 minutes or until cheese melts. Arrange remaining English muffin halves on top. Serve immediately.

> ### Micro-Tip
>
> Wrap muffins in plastic wrap and refrigerate. To reheat, remove plastic; wrap in a paper towel and place on a plate. Microwave each sandwich on Medium (50%) for 1 1/2 minutes or until warm to the touch.

Tips for Cooking Bacon in the Microwave Oven

The amount of time needed to cook bacon in the microwave depends not only on the speed of your microwave oven, but also on the thickness of the bacon and its salt, sugar and moisture content. Use a bacon rack or place bacon slices in a single layer on a large paper towel–lined plate. Cover with a paper towel to prevent splatters. Watch carefully to prevent overcooking.

Suggested times on High:
(Increase time slightly for crisp bacon)

2 slices: $1\frac{1}{2}$ to 3 minutes
4 slices: $2\frac{1}{2}$ to 5 minutes
6 slices: $3\frac{1}{2}$ to 6 minutes

Cooking bacon for a crowd:
Here's a timesaving way to cook bacon when you're serving breakfast to a crowd. Line bottom of a shallow 10-cup (2.5 L) baking dish with double thickness of paper towels. Layer bacon slices in dish allowing 5 slices per layer separated by a double sheet of paper towels. Cover with a paper towel. Microwave on High allowing for 3 to 4 minutes per layer, or until bacon is crisp. Do no more than 4 layers at a time. Check often to ensure that bacon does not overcook.

Mushroom Cheese Muffin Melt

Serves 2

These tasty open-faced melts are undeniable proof that there's more to breakfast or brunch than eggs to satisfy the tummy.

Variation

Pizza Cheese Toasts
Spread English muffins with your favorite pizza sauce and replace part of the mushrooms with thinly sliced green pepper. Use mozzarella instead of Gouda cheese.

Bacon rack (optional)
4-cup (1 L) casserole dish

4	slices bacon, halved	4
2 tsp	butter	10 mL
2 cups	thinly sliced mushrooms (about 6 oz/175 g)	500 mL
Pinch	dried oregano leaves	Pinch
	Salt and freshly ground black pepper	
Dash	Worcestershire sauce	Dash
2	English muffins, split	2
	Mayonnaise or herb cream cheese	
4	slices Gouda, Fontina, Swiss or Gruyère cheese	4

1. Place bacon on a bacon rack or paper towel–lined plate. Cover with a paper towel. Microwave on High for 3 to 5 minutes or until just crisp.

2. In casserole dish, combine butter, mushrooms and oregano. Microwave, uncovered, on High for 2 to 3 minutes, stirring once, until mushrooms are just tender. Season with salt, pepper and Worcestershire sauce.

3. Toast English muffins and spread with mayonnaise. Put 2 half slices bacon on each muffin half and top with mushrooms. Arrange 1 slice of cheese on each muffin half and place on a paper towel–lined plate.

4. Microwave, uncovered, on Medium (50%) for $1\frac{1}{2}$ to $2\frac{1}{2}$ minutes or until cheese melts. (Or arrange on a baking sheet and place under a preheated broiler for about 2 minutes or until cheese melts.) Serve immediately.

Micro-Tip

To warm sandwiches, always wrap in a paper towel to absorb excess moisture or place on a bacon rack or tray to prevent breads from getting soggy on the bottom. Also use a lower power setting such as Medium-High (70%) or Medium (50%) for even heating.

Potato and Red Pepper Frittata

A frittata is an Italian-style baked omelet with assorted vegetables. This one, with bacon and Parmesan cheese, makes a delicious brunch or light supper dish.

Tip

To bake in the oven: In Step 4, pour mixture back into quiche dish. Bake in preheated 350°F (180°C) oven for 25 to 30 minutes or until top is lightly colored and eggs are just set in center when tested with tip of a knife.

9-inch (23 cm) quiche dish or deep microwave-safe pie plate

4	slices bacon, chopped	4
1	large potato, peeled and finely diced	1
1	small red bell pepper, finely diced	1
⅔ cup	milk	150 mL
6	eggs	6
3	green onions, sliced	3
⅓ cup	freshly grated Parmesan cheese	75 mL
½ tsp	salt	2 mL
	Freshly ground black pepper	

1. In quiche dish, sprinkle bacon in a single layer. Cover with a paper towel. Microwave on High for 3 to 5 minutes or until crisp. Transfer bacon to a paper towel–lined plate. Let cool, crumble and reserve.

2. Pour off excess fat in dish. Add potatoes and red pepper. Cover with plastic wrap and turn back one corner to vent. Microwave on High for 4 to 6 minutes, stirring once, until vegetables are tender.

3. In a small glass measure, microwave milk, uncovered, on High for 1 to 1½ minutes or until hot. Crack eggs into a large bowl. Gradually whisk in hot milk until smooth. Stir in bacon bits, vegetables, green onions and Parmesan. Season with salt and pepper.

4. Pour mixture back into quiche dish. Microwave, uncovered, on Medium (50%) for new ovens and Medium-High (70%) for older or lower-wattage ovens for 12 to 16 minutes, until egg mixture is almost set in center, rotating dish twice during cooking. Let stand for 5 minutes before serving.

Spinach and Cheddar Bread Pudding

■ Here's a super brunch dish that tastes just like quiche without the hassle of making pastry. You can assemble it the night before, pop it in the microwave first to shorten the cooking time, then finish it in a regular oven.

Tip

You can replace the bacon with ½ cup (125 mL) diced ham or omit it for a vegetarian dish.

Variation

Add 1 tbsp (15 mL) butter when cooking spinach and green onions.

8-cup (2 L) casserole dish with lid
8-inch (2 L) square baking dish, well buttered

1	package (10 oz/300 g) fresh spinach	1
6	slices bacon, chopped	6
4	green onions, sliced	4
4	eggs	4
1½ cups	milk	375 mL
½ tsp	salt	2 mL
	Freshly ground black pepper and nutmeg	
4 cups	white or whole wheat bread cubes (5 to 6 slices), lightly packed	1 L
1 cup	shredded Cheddar cheese	250 mL

1. Remove any tough stems from spinach. Rinse in a sink full of cold water. Drain in a colander and pack into casserole dish. Microwave, covered, on High for 4 to 6 minutes, stirring once, until wilted. Place in colander. Using back of a wooden spoon, squeeze out as much moisture as possible. Chop finely.

2. Sprinkle bacon in same casserole dish in single layer. Cover loosely with a paper towel. Microwave on High for 4 to 6 minutes or until crisp. Transfer bacon to a paper towel–lined plate. Let cool, then crumble and set aside.

3. Drain excess fat from dish. Add spinach and green onions. Microwave, covered, on High for 3 to 5 minutes, stirring once, until tender. Let cool slightly.

4. In a bowl, beat eggs. Stir in milk, bacon and spinach mixture. Season with salt, and pepper and nutmeg to taste. Arrange bread cubes in buttered shallow baking dish. Pour spinach mixture over top. Cover with plastic wrap and refrigerate overnight.

5. Preheat oven to 350°F (180°C). Meanwhile, microwave dish (do not remove plastic wrap) on Medium (50%) for 10 to 14 minutes or until partially cooked around edges. Remove plastic and sprinkle with cheese. Finish cooking in preheated oven for 20 to 25 minutes or until top is puffed and golden and center is set when tested with tip of a sharp knife. Let stand for 5 minutes before serving.

Micro-Tip

▓ To use frozen spinach instead of fresh: Place frozen spinach in casserole dish. Microwave, covered, on High for 4 to 6 minutes, stirring once, until completely defrosted and hot. Place in colander and, using the back of a spoon, squeeze out as much moisture as possible.

Cream of Wheat with Dried Fruits

■ Cream of wheat, a classic breakfast staple, is semolina, the starchy center of the wheat kernel. Here, I've added a nutritional and flavor boost with oat or wheat bran and iron-rich dried fruits.

Tips

To make cinnamon sugar, combine 2 tbsp (25 mL) granulated sugar with $\frac{1}{2}$ tsp (2 mL) ground cinnamon.

Use any kind of dried fruits including raisins, cranberries, chopped apricots or apples.

8-cup (2 L) large glass measure or casserole dish

2 cups	milk or water (approx.)	500 mL
$\frac{1}{3}$ cup	cream of wheat	75 mL
$\frac{1}{4}$ cup	oat or wheat bran (or combination of both)	50 mL
Pinch	salt	Pinch
$\frac{1}{4}$ cup	dried fruits (see Tips, left)	50 mL
	Cinnamon sugar, brown sugar or honey to taste	

1. In glass measure, combine milk, cream of wheat, bran and salt.

2. Microwave, uncovered, on High for $3\frac{1}{2}$ to 5 minutes or until mixture just starts to thicken. Whisk well and add dried fruits. Microwave, uncovered, on High for 2 to 3 minutes, stirring once, until mixture comes to a full rolling boil and thickens.

3. Let stand for 2 minutes. Thin with milk to desired consistency and sweeten with cinnamon sugar. Spoon into 2 bowls and serve.

Oatmeal with Apples and Cranberries

Oatmeal is such a wonderful healthy breakfast. The addition of apples and dried cranberries makes it even more appealing and nourishing.

Tip

Take advantage of the speed of your microwave oven to make tasty breakfasts to start your day. Skipping breakfast may seem like a good way to save on calories, but research also shows we make up for those calories by overeating at other meals. By eating breakfast, even a simple bowl of cereal, we tend to burn more calories during the day.

4-cup (1 L) glass measure or casserole dish

$2/3$ cup	quick-cooking (not instant) rolled oats	150 mL
$1\,1/3$ cups	water or milk	325 mL
1	apple, peeled, cored and chopped	1
$1/4$ cup	dried cranberries	50 mL
Pinch	salt	Pinch
	Milk	
	Honey or brown sugar to taste	

1. In glass measure, combine oats, water, apple, cranberries and salt. Microwave, uncovered, on High for 4 to 6 minutes, stirring twice, until mixture comes to a full rolling boil and thickens. (Watch carefully to prevent mixture from boiling over.)

2. Let stand for 2 minutes. Thin with milk to desired consistency and sweeten with honey to taste. Spoon into 2 bowls and serve.

Breakfast Couscous

Serves 2

Tired of dry cereal for breakfast? Here's an interesting breakfast dish chock full of complex carbohydrates and fiber to give you a wholesome start to your day.

Tip

Dried slivered apricots, prunes, raisins and dates — whatever you have in your cupboard — are good candidates in this tasty recipe.

4-cup (1 L) casserole dish with lid

1 cup	apple juice	250 mL
1/4 cup	chopped dried fruits (see Tip, left)	50 mL
1/4 tsp	ground cinnamon	1 mL
2/3 cup	regular or whole wheat couscous	150 mL
3 tbsp	sliced unblanched almonds	45 mL
	Honey or brown sugar	
	Plain or flavored yogurt	

1. In casserole dish, combine apple juice, dried fruits and cinnamon. Microwave, covered, on High for 2$\frac{1}{2}$ to 4 minutes or until mixture comes to a full boil. Stir in couscous. Let stand, covered, for 5 minutes. Fluff with fork.

2. Stir in almonds and sweeten with honey to taste. Spoon into bowls and serve topped with a generous spoonful of yogurt. Serve either warm or cold.

Cinnamon Dried Fruit Compote

**Makes
2 cups (500 mL)**

▨ Try this delicious fruit combination for breakfast served with granola and topped with yogurt. It's also great with cottage cheese and whole grain crackers for a wholesome lunch.

Tips

Choose dried apricots, pears, prunes, halved figs, peaches and apples to vary the flavor combination. If using prunes, add halfway through cooking time since they require less time to cook.

Use your vegetable peeler to easily remove the thin outer peel of citrus fruit.

8-cup (2 L) glass measure or casserole dish with lid

1 cup	dried fruits, chopped (see Tips, left)	250 mL
2 cups	apple juice	500 mL
¼ cup	packed brown sugar	50 mL
2	strips (each 3 inches/7.5 cm) fresh lemon or orange peel (see Tips, left)	2
1	cinnamon stick, broken into 2 pieces	1

1. In glass measure, combine dried fruits, apple juice, brown sugar, lemon peel and cinnamon stick. Cover with plastic wrap and turn back one corner to vent.

2. Microwave, covered, on High for 5 to 7 minutes or until boiling. Stir and reduce heat to Medium (50%) for 5 to 8 minutes or until fruit is tender. Let stand, covered, for 10 minutes. Remove peel and cinnamon stick. Compote can be refrigerated in a covered container for up to 2 weeks.

Micro-Tip

▨ To cook or stew dried fruits: Use 1 cup (250 mL) dried fruit and add 2 cups (500 mL) water. Follow directions and microwave times in recipe.

Café au Chocolat

Here's a soothing, hot pick-me-up drink for a frosty morning. It's also great later in the day for fireside sipping after a winter outing. Try it spiked with a splash of Tia Maria, Kahlúa or a chocolate-flavored liqueur added to each mug.

Variation

Hot Chocolate
Combine sugar and cocoa powder in 4-cup (1 L) glass measure. Increase milk to 2 cups (500 mL). Blend in enough milk until smooth. Add remaining milk. Microwave on High for 3 to 4 minutes, stirring once, until piping hot. Top with whipped cream and cocoa powder, if desired.

2-cup (500 mL) glass measure

2 tbsp	unsweetened cocoa powder	25 mL
2 tbsp	granulated sugar	25 mL
1 cup	milk, divided	250 mL
1 cup	strong freshly brewed hot coffee	250 mL
	Whipped cream (optional)	
	Unsweetened cocoa powder (optional)	

1. In glass measure, combine cocoa powder and sugar. Gradually whisk in $1/4$ cup (50 mL) of the milk until smooth. Add remaining milk and microwave, uncovered, on High for $1\frac{1}{2}$ to $2\frac{1}{2}$ minutes, stirring once, until piping hot.

2. Pour hot coffee into 2 mugs and add hot chocolate. Add a spoonful of whipped cream and sprinkle with cocoa powder, if desired.

Micro-Tip

To warm up your coffee or other beverages in the microwave:
- Ensure cup or mug is microwave-safe (do not use a foam cup).
- Reheat each mug on High for 30 to 60 seconds. Continue to microwave until desired temperature.
- Do not let coffee boil or it will be bitter.
- Stir to redistribute heat uniformly.

Poultry

Honey Lemon Chicken

Serves 4

The tang of lemon combined with the sweetness of honey makes this quick and easy dish a family favorite.

8 inch (2 L) square baking dish or 9 inch (23 cm) deep microwave-safe plate

1	large clove garlic, minced	1
2 tbsp	soy sauce	25 mL
2 tbsp	liquid honey (see Micro-Tip, below)	25 mL
½ tsp	finely grated lemon zest	2 mL
2 tbsp	freshly squeezed lemon juice	25 mL
4	skinless boneless chicken breasts (1¼ lbs/625 g)	4
1½ tsp	cornstarch	7 mL
2 tbsp	chicken stock	25 mL
2	green onions, sliced	2

1. In baking dish, combine garlic, soy sauce, honey, lemon zest and juice. Microwave, uncovered, on High for 30 to 45 seconds or until sauce is fragrant.

2. Add chicken breasts to dish and spoon sauce over top. Cover with plastic wrap and turn back one corner to vent. Microwave on Medium-High (70%) for 5 to 8 minutes or until chicken is no longer pink in center, rearranging breasts once during cooking.

3. In a glass measure, blend cornstarch with stock. Turn back one corner of plastic wrap and place a plate over chicken to hold in place. Carefully pour juices into glass measure. Add green onions. Let chicken stand, covered, to keep warm.

4. Microwave sauce, uncovered, on High for 1 to 1½ minutes, stirring once, until thickened and smooth. Pour over chicken and serve.

Micro-Tip

To liquefy honey that has crystallized, remove lid from jar and microwave on High until warm and sugar crystals dissolve. (If in a plastic container, transfer to glass measure.) Time will depend on amount. For ½ cup (125 mL) honey, microwave on High for 45 to 60 seconds. Increase time for larger quantities.

How to Cook Chicken Safely in the Microwave Oven

Differences in how microwave ovens function and variations in power levels can make cooking times unreliable in recipes, especially when using older microwave ovens, whose power ratings drop with age. To ensure the safe cooking of chicken in the microwave oven, follow these recommendations.

• Cook chicken to an internal temperature of 180°F (85°C).

• Use an instant-read thermometer that registers temperatures in a very short time.

• Take several measurements through center region or through thickest portion of largest piece of chicken. All temperatures must reach the minimum temperature of 180°F (85°C).

• When cooking, cover chicken to prevent excessive loss of moisture and build up steam. Use a lid, microwave-safe plastic wrap (make sure it doesn't touch surface of chicken) or sheet of waxed or parchment paper.

• Rotate dish and rearrange pieces during cooking to promote even cooking.

Singapore Noodles with Chicken

Serve this pasta dish on a hot summer day when you want a sprightly burst of flavor but can't bear to turn on the barbecue, let alone the stovetop.

Tip

To separate rice noodles without having them make a mess in your kitchen, place the unwrapped package of noodles in a large paper bag and separate layers.

Variation

Instead of rice vermicelli, substitute 8 oz (250 g) linguine and cook in a large pot of boiling salted water on the stovetop just until tender but still firm, about 8 to 10 minutes. Drain well.

9-inch (23 cm) microwave-safe deep pie plate
8-cup (2 L) glass measure or casserole dish

3	skinless boneless chicken breasts (1 lb/500 g)	3
5 oz	rice vermicelli noodles (rice sticks) (see Tip, left)	150 g
3	carrots, peeled and cut into thin matchstick pieces	3
2 cups	snow peas, trimmed and halved	500 mL
4	green onions, sliced	4
1/4 cup	soy sauce	50 mL
2 tbsp	vegetable oil	25 mL
2 tbsp	rice vinegar	25 mL
1 tbsp	packed brown sugar	15 mL
1 tbsp	mild or medium curry paste or powder	15 mL
1	large clove garlic, minced	1
1/2 cup	chopped fresh cilantro	125 mL

1. Cut each chicken breast horizontally into 2 thin halves. Place in single layer in pie plate. Cover with lid or microwave-safe plastic wrap and turn back one corner to vent. Microwave on Medium-High (70%) for 4 to 7 minutes, rearranging once, until chicken is no longer pink in center. Let stand, covered, for 5 minutes. Slice chicken into thin strips. Rinse pie plate.

2. Place 4 cups (1 L) hot tap water in glass measure. Add vermicelli and microwave, uncovered, on High for 5 to 8 minutes or until boiling. Drain vermicelli and, using scissors, cut into 3-inch (7.5 cm) lengths.

3. In pie plate, arrange carrot strips around outside of dish and place snow peas in center. Add 2 tbsp (25 mL) water. Cover with plastic wrap and turn back one corner to vent. Microwave on High for 2 1/2 to 4 minutes or until vegetables are tender-crisp. Drain.

4. In a serving bowl, combine chicken, vermicelli, carrots, snow peas and green onions.

5. In another bowl, combine soy sauce, oil, vinegar, brown sugar, curry paste and garlic. Microwave, uncovered, on High for 30 to 60 seconds or until warm. Pour over noodle mixture and toss well. Sprinkle with cilantro. Serve warm or at room temperature.

Chicken Provençal

Serves 4

Here's a delicious, low-cal recipe that takes advantage of the speed and versatility of the microwave oven. Only one dish is needed to cook and serve, making after-dinner cleanup a breeze. Serve with rice or noodles along with a green salad to round out this menu, which takes only 30 minutes to prepare.

Tip

Supermarkets stock a wide selection of black olives. Use whatever type you prefer. My preferred choice in this recipe are wrinkled dry-cured black olives, but the saltier Greek Kalamata variety or mild-flavored canned black olives also work well.

8-cup (2 L) casserole dish with lid

1 tbsp	olive oil	15 mL
1	small onion, finely chopped	1
2	cloves garlic, minced	2
½ tsp	dried thyme leaves	2 mL
¼ tsp	fennel seeds (optional)	1 mL
1	green or yellow bell pepper, cut into thin 2-inch (5 cm) strips	1
1 cup	well-drained canned tomatoes, chopped	250 mL
⅓ cup	small black olives (see Tip, left)	75 mL
	Salt and freshly ground black pepper	
4	skinless boneless chicken breasts (1¼ lbs/625 g)	4
2 tbsp	chopped fresh parsley	25 mL

1. In casserole dish, combine oil, onion, garlic, thyme and fennel seeds. Microwave, covered, on High for 2 to 3 minutes or until onion is softened.

2. Add green pepper and tomatoes. Microwave, covered, on High for 3 to 5 minutes or until pepper strips are softened.

3. Add olives. Season with salt and pepper to taste. Arrange chicken in single layer in dish and spoon sauce over breasts.

4. Microwave, covered, on Medium-High (70%) for 6 to 9 minutes until chicken is no longer pink when cut into center, rearranging breasts once during cooking. Stir in parsley. Let stand, covered, for 5 minutes before serving.

Combo-Roasted Chicken

Use the speed of your microwave oven to reduce the time it normally takes to roast a chicken in your oven.

Preheat oven to 425°F (220°C). Place a 3-lb (1.5 kg) chicken in an 8-cup (2 L) casserole dish. Microwave, covered, on High for 10 to 14 minutes or until chicken is partially cooked. Using two spatulas, transfer chicken to a shallow roasting pan. Place in oven and roast for 30 minutes, basting occasionally with pan juices, until meat thermometer registers 180°F (85°C).

Streamlined Chicken Stew

Looking for an easy-on-the-budget recipe? Here's a main-course supper dish that calls for chicken thighs. Instead of 1½ hours of slow simmering in a conventional oven, this tasty stew takes only about a third of the time to cook in the microwave.

Tip

Fines herbes are a combination of tarragon, parsley and chives. Or use Italian seasoning instead.

12-cup (3 L) casserole dish with lid

1 tbsp	butter	15 mL
1	large onion, halved lengthwise and thinly sliced	1
3	cloves garlic, cut into slivers	3
2	stalks celery, sliced	2
1½ tsp	dried fines herbes (see Tip, left)	7 mL
¼ cup	all-purpose flour	50 mL
1 tsp	salt	5 mL
	Freshly ground black pepper	
1 cup	chicken stock	250 mL
8	skinless chicken thighs (2 lbs/1 kg)	8
1	package (1 lb/500 g) whole baby carrots	1
1½ cups	frozen green beans	375 mL

1. In casserole dish, combine butter, onion, garlic, celery and fines herbes. Microwave, covered, on High for 3 to 5 minutes or until onion is softened.

2. In a bowl, combine flour, salt, and pepper to taste. Coat chicken on all sides in flour mixture. Arrange in single layer in casserole dish on top of vegetables.

3. Stir stock into whatever flour mixture remains in bowl until smooth. Pour mixture over chicken and top with carrots. Microwave, covered, on High for 8 to 10 minutes or until boiling.

4. Turn chicken pieces over and rearrange in dish. Reduce power to Medium (50%) and cook, covered, for 10 minutes longer. Add beans and cook, covered, on Medium (50%) for 5 to 10 minutes longer or until juices run clear when chicken is pierced with a knife and vegetables are tender. Let stand, covered, for 10 minutes, before serving.

Micro-Tip

To determine if chicken is thoroughly cooked when microwaved, cook chicken to an internal temperature of 180°F (85°C). Cut into chicken to make sure it is no longer pink inside and juices run clear. Make a cut near the bone area as with chicken thighs or legs — meat should not be pink and come away from the bone easily.

Defrosting and Reheating Casseroles

■ Most casseroles, stews, pasta dishes and sauces, and hearty main-course soups are ideal to prepare ahead and freeze then reheat in the microwave.

To reduce defrosting and reheating time, place frozen dish or container in the refrigerator to partially thaw overnight. Follow directions in your oven manual for recommended defrosting times and power levels, or use the sensor defrost and reheat feature on your microwave oven.

For casseroles that cannot be stirred (such as lasagna):
As a general guideline for manual defrosting, defrost at a lower power setting such as Medium (50%) or Medium-Low/Defrost (30%) and rotate dish occasionally to promote even defrosting.

For casseroles, stews, soups and sauces that can be stirred:
If in a plastic storage container, rinse under hot water to loosen contents and transfer to a microwave-safe dish. As a guideline, start defrosting on High and once food can be separated, reduce power to Medium (50%) or Medium-Low/Defrost (30%) to allow for even defrosting.

To reheat: Cover dish with lid or vented plastic wrap and use the sensor reheat feature, or for manual reheating, microwave on Medium-High (70%), stirring once or twice, until piping hot.

Chicken Paprika

Moist, tender chicken cooked in the microwave is a popular choice for fast and easy dinners. Convenient boneless chicken thighs are a less expensive alternative to pricey chicken breasts in this classic dish. Toss sauce with noodles and serve with a salad or green vegetable, such as broccoli, for a dinner that's ready in about 30 minutes.

Tips

I recommend using Hungarian paprika if you can find it, or the Spanish kind available in supermarkets is also fine.

To get the best texture and flavor, use full-fat (regular) sour cream.

This dish freezes well. Place in covered storage container and freeze for up to 2 months.

8-cup (2 L) casserole dish with lid

1 tbsp	vegetable oil	15 mL
1	onion, halved lengthwise and thinly sliced	1
2 cups	quartered mushrooms (about 6 oz/175 g)	500 mL
2 tsp	paprika (see Tips, left)	10 mL
½ tsp	dried thyme leaves	2 mL
2 tbsp	tomato paste	25 mL
2 tbsp	all-purpose flour	25 mL
½ cup	chicken stock	125 mL
1 lb	skinless boneless chicken thighs or breasts, cut into 1-inch (2.5 cm) cubes	500 g
¾ tsp	salt	4 mL
	Freshly ground black pepper	
⅓ cup	sour cream (see Tips, left)	75 mL

1. In casserole dish, combine oil, onion, mushrooms, paprika, thyme and tomato paste. Microwave, covered, on High for 4 to 6 minutes, stirring once, until vegetables are tender.

2. In a bowl, blend flour with chicken stock until smooth. Stir into onion mixture along with chicken pieces. Season with salt, and pepper to taste.

3. Microwave, covered, on High for 6 to 9 minutes, stirring twice, until chicken is no longer pink inside. Stir in sour cream. Let stand, covered, for 3 minutes before serving.

Egg Tomato Muffin Melt with Bacon (page 46)

Overleaf: Beef Cobbler (page 74)

Hawaiian Chicken

If you love the sweetness of pineapple with chicken, this '50s-style dish, updated with snappy fresh ginger and curry, is definitely for you. Serve it over rice and accompany with steamed broccoli.

Tip

One of the newest convenience products in supermarkets is curry paste, usually stocked in the international food section. Like curry powders, curry pastes are a distinct blend of many spices and add a rich, robust flavor to dishes. They can be mild or very hot depending on the style of curry paste that you buy, so taste first before adding to a dish.

8-cup (2 L) casserole dish with lid

1 tbsp	vegetable oil	15 mL
1	onion, chopped	1
1 tbsp	minced fresh gingerroot	15 mL
1 tbsp	mild curry paste or powder (see Tip, left)	15 mL
1	can (14 oz/398 mL) unsweetened pineapple chunks, drained, juice reserved	1
1 tbsp	cornstarch	15 mL
1 lb	skinless boneless chicken thighs, cut into 1-inch (2.5 cm) cubes	500 g
1/3 cup	chicken stock	75 mL
2 tbsp	tomato paste	25 mL
1/2 tsp	salt	2 mL
	Freshly ground black pepper	
1	red or green bell pepper, cut into thin 1 1/2-inch (4 cm) strips	1

1. In casserole dish, combine oil, onion, ginger and curry paste. Microwave, covered, on High for 2 to 3 minutes or until onion is softened.

2. In a small bowl, blend cornstarch with 1/2 cup (125 mL) of the pineapple juice, setting aside remaining juice for another use.

3. Stir cornstarch mixture into onion mixture along with chicken pieces, stock, tomato paste, salt, and pepper to taste. Microwave, covered, on High for 5 to 7 minutes, stirring once, until chicken is no longer pink inside and sauce thickens.

4. Stir in pineapple chunks and red pepper. Microwave, covered, on High for 3 to 5 minutes, stirring once, until pepper strips are tender-crisp. Let stand, covered, for 3 minutes before serving.

Chicken Provençal (page 61)

Quick Chicken Cacciatore

Serves 4

This streamlined chicken dish is ready to serve in the time it takes to cook pasta on the stovetop.

Tip

Depending on amount of seasoning in the pasta sauce you're using, up the amount of herbs, such as basil or oregano, and a pinch of hot pepper flakes for a flavor boost.

8-cup (2 L) casserole dish with lid

1 lb	skinless boneless chicken thighs, cut into 1-inch (2.5 cm) cubes	500 g
1 tbsp	olive oil	15 mL
1	small onion, chopped	1
1	red or green bell pepper, cut into thin 1½-inch (4 cm) strips	1
½ tsp	dried basil leaves	2 mL
¼ tsp	dried thyme leaves	1 mL
½ tsp	salt	2 mL
	Freshly ground black pepper	
2 cups	tomato pasta sauce (see Tip, left)	500 mL

1. In casserole dish, combine chicken, oil, onion, red pepper, basil, thyme, salt, and pepper to taste. Microwave, covered, on High for 5 to 8 minutes, stirring once, until chicken is no longer pink inside.

2. Stir in pasta sauce. Microwave, covered, on High for 4 to 7 minutes, stirring once, until piping hot. Let stand, covered, for 3 minutes before serving.

Micro-Tip

Because of the shorter microwave cooking times, dried herbs often don't have the chance to impart a depth of flavor to a dish as when cooked conventionally. To get the most flavor from dried herbs, always add them at the beginning of cooking, along with oil and onions.

Creole Chicken and Rice Bake

■ Here's an enticing way to cook chicken that's always a popular choice for a hearty main-course family supper.

10-cup (3 L) casserole dish with lid

1 tbsp	vegetable oil	15 mL
1	onion, finely chopped	1
¾ cup	chopped celery	175 mL
2	cloves garlic, minced	2
½ tsp	dried thyme leaves	2 mL
½ tsp	dried oregano leaves	2 mL
½ tsp	salt	2 mL
Pinch	hot pepper flakes	Pinch
1 cup	long-grain white rice	250 mL
1	large tomato, seeded and chopped	1
1⅓ cups	chicken stock	325 mL
1 lb	skinless boneless chicken, cut into 1-inch (2.5 cm) cubes (about 8 thighs or 4 breasts)	500 g
1	large green bell pepper, chopped	1

1. In casserole dish, combine oil, onion, celery, garlic, thyme, oregano, salt and hot pepper flakes. Microwave, covered, on High for 4 to 6 minutes, stirring once, until vegetables are tender.

2. Add rice, tomato and chicken stock. Microwave, covered, on High for 4 to 6 minutes or until boiling.

3. Bury chicken pieces in rice. Microwave, covered, on Medium-High (70%) for 10 to 14 minutes or until rice is almost tender. Stir in green pepper. Continue to microwave on Medium-High (70%) for 4 to 8 minutes longer or until chicken is tender and most of liquid has been absorbed. Let stand, covered, for 10 minutes before serving.

Chicken Caesar Wrap

Makes 6 wraps

■ I've taken the classic chicken Caesar salad and transformed it into a popular wrap for a great-tasting tote-along lunch or dinner sandwich.

Tip

Instead of cooking chicken breasts, use 2 cups (500 mL) diced cooked chicken or turkey instead.

9-inch (23 cm) microwave-safe pie plate
Bacon rack (optional)

2	large skinless boneless chicken breasts (12 oz/375 g)	2
6	slices bacon	6
1/2 cup	light mayonnaise	125 mL
1 tsp	anchovy paste	5 mL
1 tsp	Dijon mustard	5 mL
1 tbsp	freshly squeezed lemon juice	15 mL
1/4 cup	drained oil-packed sun-dried tomatoes, chopped	50 mL
2 tbsp	shredded Parmesan cheese	25 mL
	Freshly ground black pepper	
6	large (9 inch/23 cm) flour tortillas	6
6 cups	shredded romaine lettuce	1.5 L

1. Slice chicken breasts horizontally into 2 thin pieces each. Place in pie plate in single layer. Cover with plastic wrap and turn back one corner to vent. Microwave on Medium (50%) for 4 to 6 minutes, until no longer pink. Let stand, covered, for 3 minutes. Cut into thin strips.

2. Place bacon on bacon rack or on large plate lined with a double layer of paper towels. Loosely cover with another layer of paper towels. Microwave on High for 4 to 6 minutes or until cooked and crisp. Let cool, then crumble.

3. In a bowl, combine mayonnaise, anchovy paste, mustard and lemon juice. Add chicken, bacon bits, sun-dried tomatoes and Parmesan cheese. Season with pepper.

4. Spread about 1/3 cup (75 mL) of chicken filling over bottom half of each tortilla. Top with 1 cup (250 mL) shredded lettuce. Fold 1-inch (2.5 cm) of the right and left sides of tortilla over filling. Starting from bottom, roll tortillas around filling to enclose.

5. Place 3 sandwiches at a time, seam side down, on a paper towel–lined plate. Microwave on Medium-High (70%) for 1 to 1 1/2 minutes or until slightly warm to the touch. Repeat with remaining wraps. Serve immediately.

Micro-Tip

■ To make ahead, complete recipe to Step 4. Wrap sandwiches individually in plastic wrap and store in the refrigerator for up to 1 day. To warm individual wraps, remove plastic and wrap in a paper towel. Reheat on Medium-High (70%) for 30 to 45 seconds.

Swiss Cheese and Smoked Turkey Melt

Serves 1

■ Use a variety of whole grain breads and your microwave to create fast supper sandwiches. Try any one of the specialty mustards available in stores and delis. Or spread bread with flavored cream cheeses such as herb and garlic.

2	slices 6-grain bread or other firm-textured bread such as pumpernickel or rye	2
	Dijon or grainy mustard	
2	thin slices smoked turkey	2
1	slice Swiss cheese, such as Gruyère	1
2	tomato slices	2

1. Spread one bread slice with mustard. Layer with smoked turkey, cheese and tomato slices. Top with second bread slice.

2. Wrap sandwich in paper towel and place on plate. Microwave on Medium (50%) for 45 seconds to $1\frac{1}{2}$ minutes or until cheese begins to melt.

Micro-Tip

■ To warm bread or buns in the microwave, wrap in paper napkin or paper towel or place directly in cloth or paper napkin–lined wicker basket. Paper or cloth absorbs moisture and prevents bread from getting soggy and hard. Microwave soft rolls and buns on Medium (50%) and more dense breads on Medium-High (70%) just until bread feels warm to the touch. Times vary with types of bread. Heat only for a short time and check often to prevent overheating.

Amazing Turkey Enchiladas

▪ Instead of turning chicken or turkey leftovers into a week's worth of cold sandwiches, whip up this fast-fix dinner with loads of family appeal.

Tip
You can assemble this dish a day ahead of baking. Cover dish with plastic wrap and refrigerate for up to 1 day. Top with salsa and cheese prior to heating in the microwave.

Variation
Use $1\frac{1}{2}$ cups (375 mL) small cooked shrimp instead of turkey or chicken.

13-by 9-inch (3 L) baking dish, greased (see Micro-Tip, below)

$\frac{1}{2}$ cup	cream cheese (4 oz/125 g), cubed	125 mL
$\frac{1}{2}$ cup	plain yogurt or sour cream	125 mL
2 cups	cooked turkey or chicken, cut into thin strips	500 mL
3	green onions, sliced	3
2	tomatoes, seeded and diced	2
$\frac{1}{4}$ cup	chopped fresh cilantro or parsley	50 mL
6	large (9-inch/23 cm) flour tortillas	6
$1\frac{1}{2}$ cups	mild or medium salsa	375 mL
1 cup	shredded Cheddar or Monterey Jack cheese	250 mL
	Chopped fresh cilantro (optional)	

1. Place cream cheese in a large bowl. Microwave, uncovered, on Medium (50%) for 45 to 60 seconds, until softened. Stir well. Stir in yogurt, turkey, green onions, tomatoes and cilantro.

2. Spread about one-sixth of the turkey mixture down center of each tortilla and roll up. Arrange tortillas in single layer, seam side down, in baking dish. Spread with salsa. Cover dish with waxed paper. Microwave on Medium-High (70%) for 7 to 9 minutes or until heated through.

3. Sprinkle with cheese. Microwave, uncovered, on High for 1 minute or until cheese melts. Sprinkle with extra chopped cilantro, if desired.

Micro-Tip

▪ Some of today's smaller-size microwave ovens cannot hold a 13-by 9-inch (3 L) baking dish. Instead, use two 9-inch (23 cm) microwave-safe pie plates or 8-inch (2 L) square baking dishes or 11-by 7-inch (2 L) baking dishes. Microwave each batch on Medium-High (70%) for 5 to 7 minutes.

Beef, Pork and Lamb

Spicy Asian Beef with Peppers and Snow Peas

The microwave oven is such a great device, not only for the obvious reason that it cooks food fast, but because it allows you to create recipes that don't require any added fat in the cooking. This low-cal stir-fry is just one tasty example.

8-cup (2 L) casserole dish with lid

1/3 cup	beef stock	75 mL
2 tbsp	black bean sauce	25 mL
2 tbsp	soy sauce	25 mL
1	large clove garlic, minced	1
1 tbsp	minced fresh gingerroot	15 mL
1 tsp	granulated sugar	5 mL
1 tsp	Asian chili paste	5 mL
1 tbsp	cornstarch	15 mL
1 lb	boneless beef sirloin steak, trimmed	500 g
2 cups	snow peas, ends trimmed	500 mL
1	red bell pepper, cut into thin 2-inch (5 cm) strips	1

1. In casserole dish, combine stock, black bean sauce, soy sauce, garlic, ginger, sugar and chili paste. Stir in cornstarch until smooth. Microwave, uncovered, on High for 1 1/2 to 2 minutes, stirring once, until sauce is very thick.

2. Slice meat on the diagonal into very thin strips. Toss beef strips with sauce in casserole dish. Microwave, uncovered, on High for 2 1/2 to 4 minutes or until beef is partially cooked.

3. Arrange snow peas and red pepper on top of beef. Microwave, covered, on High for 3 to 5 minutes or until vegetables are tender-crisp. Stir vegetables into beef mixture. Let stand, covered, for 2 minutes.

Micro-Tip

Steaming vegetables such as broccoli, bell peppers or snow peas in the microwave is a great way to eliminate the use of butter or oil needed for sautéing vegetables in stir-fries on the stovetop. Place vegetables in an 9-inch (23 cm) deep microwave-safe pie plate and arrange ones that cook the quickest in the middle of the dish. Add 1 tbsp (15 mL) water per cup (250 mL) of vegetables. Cover with lid, microwave-safe plate or plastic wrap with one corner turned back to vent. Microwave on High for 30 to 45 seconds per cup (250 mL) of vegetables or until brightly colored and tender-crisp. Drain and add to stir-fry.

Herb Beef Ragout with Vegetables

Serves 4

Warm up on cold nights with comforting and nourishing stews. Like most stewed dishes, you'll find that their flavors improve when refrigerated overnight and reheated the next day. This stew is especially good served with noodles or mashed potatoes.

Tip

If desired, you can first brown the beef cubes in 1 tbsp (15 mL) olive oil in a nonstick skillet on the stovetop over high heat for a richer color. Instead of tossing the flour with meat, blend flour into stock until smooth.

8-cup (2 L) casserole dish with lid

1 tbsp	olive oil	15 mL
1	onion, chopped	1
2	cloves garlic, minced	2
2	stalks celery, chopped	2
1 tsp	dried Italian seasoning	5 mL
1 lb	stewing beef or veal, cut into 1-inch (2.5 cm) cubes	500 g
2 tbsp	all-purpose flour	25 mL
1 cup	canned tomatoes, chopped	250 mL
3/4 cup	beef stock	175 mL
2 tbsp	fancy molasses	25 mL
1 tbsp	balsamic vinegar	15 mL
3/4 tsp	salt	4 mL
	Freshly ground black pepper	
4 cups	frozen Italian-style mixed vegetables	1 L

1. In casserole dish, combine oil, onion, garlic, celery and Italian seasoning. Microwave, covered, on High for 3 to 5 minutes or until vegetables are softened.

2. In a bowl, toss meat with flour. Add to casserole with tomatoes, stock, molasses, vinegar, salt and pepper. Microwave, covered, on High for 7 to 10 minutes or until boiling. Stir well. Microwave, covered, on Medium (50%) for 20 to 25 minutes longer, stirring once, until meat is tender.

3. Add frozen vegetables and microwave, covered, on High for 7 to 10 minutes or until vegetables are tender. Let stand, covered, for 5 minutes before serving.

Micro-Tip

Small batch stews work best in the microwave oven. Doubling the recipe can take as long to cook conventionally so consider preparing a large batch of stew the old-fashioned way on your stovetop or in your oven.

Beef Cobbler

This is one of those simple but comforting one-dish meals made with economical ground beef that everyone loves. I often make the meat base ahead and tuck it away in the freezer, ready to defrost and reheat quickly in the microwave oven while I preheat the oven and make the easy biscuit topping.

Tip

What to do with leftover tomato paste once you've opened a can? I place tablespoonfuls (15 mL) on a waxed paper–lined plate, and freeze until solid, then transfer frozen portions to a container and store in the freezer to add to sauces. Tomato paste sold in convenient tubes is also ideal to have on hand. Just measure what you need and return the tube to the fridge for future use.

Preheat oven to 400°F (200°C)
8-cup (2 L) casserole dish with lid

1 lb	lean ground beef or veal	500 g
1	onion, finely chopped	1
1 cup	sliced mushrooms	250 mL
1	large garlic clove, minced	1
1/2 tsp	dried thyme leaves	2 mL
2 tbsp	all-purpose flour	25 mL
1 1/4 cups	beef stock, divided	300 mL
2 tbsp	tomato paste (see Tip, left)	25 mL
1 tbsp	Worcestershire sauce	15 mL
1/2 tsp	salt	2 mL
	Freshly ground black pepper	
1 cup	frozen peas	250 mL
CRUST		
1 1/2 cups	biscuit mix	375 mL
3/4 cup	shredded Cheddar cheese, divided	175 mL
6 tbsp	milk (approx.)	90 mL

1. Crumble beef into casserole dish. Microwave, **uncovered**, on High for 5 to 7 minutes, until beef is no longer pink, stirring twice and using a fork to break up meat lumps. Drain off any excess fat in dish.

2. Add onion, mushrooms, garlic and thyme to beef in casserole dish. Microwave, covered, on High for 3 to 5 minutes or until vegetables are softened.

3. Place flour in a bowl and blend in 1/3 cup (75 mL) of the stock until smooth. Stir into beef along with remaining stock, tomato paste, Worcestershire sauce, salt, and pepper to taste. Microwave, covered, on High for 4 to 6 minutes or until sauce boils and thickens. Stir in peas.

4. *Crust:* In a bowl, combine biscuit mix and half of the cheese. Using a fork, stir in enough milk to make a soft, sticky dough. Turn out onto a lightly floured board and shape into a ball. Pat dough into a circle or square large enough to fit casserole dish.

5. Place dough on top of warm meat mixture. Sprinkle top with remaining cheese. Bake in preheated oven for 20 to 25 minutes or until top is golden.

Micro-Tip

Pastry- or biscuit-topped casseroles, as in this recipe, do not brown or cook properly in the microwave oven and are best baked conventionally in your oven.

Italian Beef Heroes

Easy-to-prepare sandwiches are always welcome for a great-tasting fast dinner. Make them with leftover grilled steak or store-bought deli roast beef.

Variations

Salsa Beef Heroes
Substitute 3/4 to 1 cup (175 to 250 mL) thick salsa for the tomato pasta sauce.

Use sliced cooked sausages, roast turkey or chicken instead of beef.

4-cup (1 L) casserole dish with lid

1 tbsp	olive oil	15 mL
1	green or red bell pepper, cut into thin 1½-inch (4 cm) strips	1
1	small onion, cut into thin wedges	1
1	large clove garlic, minced	1
½ tsp	dried oregano leaves	2 mL
¼ tsp	hot pepper flakes	1 mL
1½ cups	thinly sliced cooked steak or 6 oz (175 g) deli roast beef, cut into strips	375 mL
1 cup	thick tomato pasta sauce	250 mL
4	crusty rolls (7 inches/18 cm long)	4
6 oz	thinly sliced mild provolone or mozzarella cheese	175 g

1. In casserole dish, combine oil, green pepper, onion, garlic, oregano and hot pepper flakes. Microwave, covered, on High for 3 to 5 minutes or until vegetables are softened. Stir in beef and pasta sauce. Microwave, covered, on High for 2 to 3 minutes, stirring once, until piping hot.

2. Cut rolls along one side but not all the way through. Open up. Layer with cheese slices. Place 2 sandwiches at time on a paper towel–lined plate. Microwave, uncovered, on Medium (50%) for 1 to 1½ minutes or until cheese melts. Spoon ½ cup (125 mL) of the hot beef mixture into each roll. Serve immediately.

Micro-Tip

Prepare sandwich filling ahead, cover and refrigerate for up to 2 days. When ready to prepare, layer rolls with cheese. Spoon in beef filling. Wrap in paper towels and microwave on Medium (50%) for 2 to 3 minutes for 2 rolls, or 1 to 1½ minutes for 1 roll, or until heated through.

Tex-Mex Beef and Rice Casserole

Serves 4 to 6

■ Here's a terrific make-ahead casserole dish that easily reheats in the microwave in about the same time as it takes to toss a salad and set the table.

8-cup (2 L) casserole dish with lid

1 lb	lean ground beef	500 g
1	onion, finely chopped	1
2	large cloves garlic, minced	2
4 tsp	chili powder	20 mL
1 tsp	dried oregano leaves	5 mL
½ tsp	salt	2 mL
	Freshly ground black pepper	
3 cups	cooked long-grain white or brown rice (about 1 cup/250 mL uncooked) (see Micro-Tip, below)	750 mL
1½ cups	fresh, frozen or canned corn kernels	375 mL
1½ cups	medium salsa	375 mL
1 cup	shredded Cheddar cheese	250 mL

1. Crumble beef into casserole dish and microwave, uncovered, on High for 5 to 7 minutes, until no longer pink, stirring twice and using a fork to break up meat lumps. Drain off any excess fat in dish.

2. Add onion, garlic, chili powder, oregano, salt and pepper to beef in casserole dish. Microwave, covered, on High for 3 to 5 minutes or until onion is softened. Transfer to a bowl and stir in rice.

3. In another bowl, combine corn and salsa. In casserole dish, layer half the beef mixture, then half the corn mixture. Repeat layers. (Can be made ahead to this point and refrigerated for up to 1 day.)

4. Microwave, covered, on High for 12 to 16 minutes (5 to 7 minutes longer if refrigerated) or until piping hot in center. Sprinkle with cheese. Microwave, uncovered, for 1 to 2 minutes or until cheese melts.

Micro-Tip

■ To cook white rice: In an 8-cup (2 L) casserole dish, combine 2 cups (500 mL) water, 1 cup (250 mL) long-grain white rice and ½ tsp (2 mL) salt. Microwave, covered, on High for 4 to 6 minutes or until boiling. Reduce to Medium (50%) for 10 to 14 minutes or until most of the liquid is absorbed. Let stand for 10 minutes. Makes 3 cups (750 mL) rice.

To cook brown rice: see page 111.

So Easy Chili

Handy cans of chili-spiced stewed tomatoes are a great base for this tasty vegetable-packed chili. Serve with crusty bread and tossed salad.

Variation

Ground chicken or turkey can be used instead of ground beef.

12-cup (3 L) casserole dish with lid

1 lb	lean ground beef	500 g
1	onion, chopped	1
2	large cloves garlic, minced	2
1 tsp	dried oregano leaves	5 mL
1 tsp	ground cumin	5 mL
1	large green bell pepper, chopped	1
1	zucchini, quartered lengthwise and thickly sliced	1
2	cans (each 19 oz/540 mL) chili-style stewed tomatoes, including juice	2
1	can (19 oz/540 mL) red kidney beans, drained and rinsed	1
	Shredded Cheddar cheese (optional)	

1. Crumble ground beef into casserole dish. Microwave, uncovered, on High for 5 to 7 minutes, until no longer pink, stirring twice and using a fork to break up meat lumps. Drain off any excess fat in dish.

2. Add onion, garlic, oregano and cumin to beef in casserole dish. Microwave, covered, on High for 3 to 5 minutes or until onion is softened.

3. Stir in green pepper, zucchini, tomatoes with juice and kidney beans. Microwave, covered, on High for 10 to 15 minutes, stirring once, until vegetables are tender. Let stand, covered, for 5 minutes before serving. Ladle into bowls and sprinkle with cheese, if desired.

Chili Sloppy Joes

<table>
<tr><td colspan="3">8-cup (2 L) casserole dish with lid</td></tr>
<tr><td>1 lb</td><td>lean ground beef</td><td>500 g</td></tr>
<tr><td>1</td><td>small onion, finely chopped</td><td>1</td></tr>
<tr><td>1</td><td>clove garlic, minced</td><td>1</td></tr>
<tr><td>1½ tsp</td><td>chili powder</td><td>7 mL</td></tr>
<tr><td>½ tsp</td><td>dried oregano leaves</td><td>2 mL</td></tr>
<tr><td></td><td>Freshly ground black pepper</td><td></td></tr>
<tr><td>1</td><td>can (7½ oz /213 mL) tomato sauce</td><td>1</td></tr>
<tr><td>½ cup</td><td>medium salsa</td><td>125 mL</td></tr>
<tr><td>4</td><td>large Kaiser rolls, split, and toasted, if desired</td><td>4</td></tr>
<tr><td>1 cup</td><td>shredded mozzarella or Cheddar cheese</td><td>250 mL</td></tr>
</table>

Makes 4 sandwiches

■ Eat these popular meaty sandwiches for supper with a knife and fork or serve them burger-style, topped with sliced tomato, lettuce and additional salsa.

Variation

Chili Sloppy Joe Burritos Spread each of 6 large flour tortillas with 2 tbsp (25 mL) spreadable cream cheese. (Use flavored cream cheese, such as roasted red pepper, if desired.) Spread with ⅓ cup (75 mL) Chili Sloppy Joe mixture. Sprinkle with chopped tomato, green pepper and shredded cheese, if desired. Fold 1 inch (2.5 cm) of the right and left sides of tortilla over filling. Starting from bottom, roll tortillas around filling. Place 3 sandwiches at a time on a paper towel–lined plate. Microwave on Medium-High (70%) for 1½ to 2 minutes or until slightly warm to the touch. Repeat with remaining wraps.

1. Crumble ground beef into casserole dish. Microwave, uncovered, on High for 5 to 7 minutes, until no longer pink, stirring twice and using a fork to break up meat lumps. Drain off any excess fat in dish.

2. Add onion, garlic, chili powder, oregano and pepper to beef in casserole. Microwave, covered, on High for 3 to 5 minutes or until onion is softened.

3. Stir in tomato sauce and salsa. Microwave, covered, on High for 4 to 6 minutes, stirring once, until piping hot and flavors are blended.

4. Spread both sides of rolls generously with beef mixture. Sprinkle with cheese. Place 2 rolls at a time on paper towel–lined plate. Microwave, uncovered, on Medium (50%) for 1 to 1½ minutes or until cheese is melted. Repeat with remaining sandwiches. Increase time slightly if filling has been made ahead and refrigerated. Serve immediately.

Micro-Tip

■ This is a handy sandwich filling to have tucked away in the freezer for fast impromptu meals. Refrigerate filling for 3 days or freeze for up to 2 months. It also makes great sandwiches to take to school or work when there is a microwave on hand. To reheat, wrap sandwich in paper towel and microwave on Medium (50%) for 1 to 1½ minutes.

Sweet-and-Sour Meatballs with Vegetables

Use convenient and economical frozen vegetables and packaged cooked meatballs, also available in the frozen food section of your supermarket, to cut down on the time it takes to prepare weekday suppers. This dish is very good served with rice. Start by microwaving the rice then assemble the ingredients for this dish.

4-cup (1 L) casserole dish with lid
8-cup (2 L) casserole dish with lid

1 lb	frozen cooked meatballs (about 36)	500 g
2 tbsp	beef stock or water	25 mL
SAUCE		
1	can (14 oz/398 mL) unsweetened pineapple chunks, drained, juice reserved	1
⅓ cup	soy sauce	75 mL
¼ cup	packed brown sugar	50 mL
1 tbsp	minced fresh gingerroot	15 mL
¼ cup	cider vinegar	50 mL
2 tbsp	cornstarch	25 mL
4 cups	mixed frozen vegetables, such as cauliflower, broccoli and carrots	1 L

1. Place meatballs in 4-cup (1 L) casserole dish and add stock. Microwave, covered, on Medium (50%) for 5 to 8 minutes, stirring once, until defrosted and heated through. Set aside.

2. *Sauce:* Measure pineapple juice (there should be ¾ cup/175 mL juice). Add additional water, if necessary. In 8-cup (2 L) casserole dish, combine pineapple juice, soy sauce, brown sugar, ginger and vinegar. Blend in cornstarch until smooth. Microwave, uncovered, on High for 3 to 5 minutes, stirring once, until sauce comes to a boil and thickens.

3. Stir in frozen vegetables. Microwave, covered, on High for 5 to 7 minutes, stirring once, until vegetables are almost tender.

4. Stir in meatballs with stock and pineapple chunks. Microwave, covered, on High for 3 to 5 minutes or until piping hot. Serve with rice.

Herb Pork and Rice with Cranberries

Serves 4

Here's an updated version of a pork and rice casserole when the pork is browned in a skillet on the stovetop for added flavor and then finished in the microwave oven. Serve with red cabbage or coleslaw.

8-cup (2 L) casserole dish with lid
4-cup (1 L) glass measure

6 to 8	thin boneless pork chops, well trimmed (1 lb/500 g)	6 to 8
½ tsp	dried thyme leaves	2 mL
	Salt and freshly ground black pepper	
1 tbsp	vegetable oil	15 mL
1 tbsp	butter	15 mL
1	large onion, chopped	1
1 tsp	crumbled dried sage	5 mL
1 cup	long-grain white rice	250 mL
¼ cup	dried cranberries	50 mL
1 cup	apple juice	250 mL
1 cup	chicken stock	250 mL
1 tbsp	Dijon mustard	15 mL
½ tsp	salt	2 mL

1. Season pork with thyme, salt and pepper. In a large nonstick skillet, heat oil over medium-high heat and cook pork for about 1 minute per side until lightly colored. Leave pork in skillet and remove from heat.

2. In casserole dish, combine butter, onion and sage. Microwave, covered, on High for 3 to 4 minutes or until onion is softened. Stir in rice and cranberries. Arrange pork chops in overlapping circle on top of rice mixture.

3. In glass measure, combine pan juices from pork, apple juice, stock, mustard and salt. Microwave, uncovered, on High for 3½ to 5 minutes or until boiling. Stir well.

4. Pour over pork chops in casserole dish. Microwave, covered, on High for 3 to 5 minutes or until liquid returns to a boil. Reduce to Medium (50%) and microwave for 10 to 14 minutes or until liquid is absorbed. Let stand, covered, for 10 minutes before serving.

Spareribs with Orange Soy Sauce

Get out the napkins when serving these succulent ribs, which are always a family favorite at dinnertime.

Tip

Sauce can be made ahead and stored in a covered container in refrigerator for up to 2 weeks.

2-cup (500 mL) glass measure
12-cup (3 L) casserole dish with lid

ORANGE SOY SAUCE

½ cup	orange juice	125 mL
⅓ cup	orange marmalade	75 mL
¼ cup	soy sauce	50 mL
1 tbsp	balsamic vinegar	15 mL
2	cloves garlic, minced	2
1 tbsp	minced fresh gingerroot	15 mL
1½ tsp	cornstarch	7 mL
3 lbs	pork spareribs	1.5 kg

1. *Sauce:* In glass measure, combine orange juice, marmalade, soy sauce, balsamic vinegar, garlic, ginger and cornstarch until smooth. Microwave, uncovered, on High for 2 to 3 minutes or until sauce comes to a boil and thickens. Let cool.

2. Cut pork into 3-rib sections. Place in casserole dish with ½ cup (125 mL) water. Microwave, covered, on High for 4 to 6 minutes. Reduce to Medium (50%) and microwave for 14 to 20 minutes, turning once, until ribs are cooked through.

3. *To barbecue:* Preheat barbecue grill to medium. Brush ribs liberally with sauce and place on preheated greased barbecue grill. Grill for 15 to 20 minutes, turning ribs often and brushing with additional sauce, until nicely glazed and fork-tender.

4. *To bake:* Preheat oven to 350°F (180°C). Place ribs on foil-lined baking sheet. Brush liberally with sauce. Bake in preheated oven for about 35 minutes, brushing occasionally with sauce, until spareribs are nicely glazed.

5. Cut into individual ribs and serve accompanied with any remaining sauce.

Braised Cabbage with Ham and Cheese

If you find shredding cabbage too time-consuming, pick up a package of coleslaw mix and use it instead in this streamlined recipe. Serve over pasta, if desired.

12-cup (3 L) casserole dish with lid

1 tbsp	vegetable oil	15 mL
1	small onion, thinly sliced	1
2	cloves garlic, minced	2
1 tsp	dried oregano leaves	5 mL
1 tsp	ground cumin	5 mL
6 cups	shredded cabbage, lightly packed, or 1 lb (500 g) packaged coleslaw mix	1.5 L
1	can (19 oz/540 mL) chili-style stewed tomatoes, including juice	1
1½ cups	cubed smoked ham or firm tofu (½-inch/1 cm cubes)	375 mL
1 cup	shredded Cheddar cheese	250 mL

1. In casserole dish, combine oil, onion, garlic, oregano and cumin. Microwave, covered, on High for 2 to 3 minutes or until onion is softened. Add cabbage and tomatoes with juice. Microwave, covered, on High for 10 to 14 minutes, stirring once, until cabbage is tender.

2. Stir in ham. Microwave, covered, on High for 2 to 3 minutes longer or until heated through.

3. Sprinkle with cheese and microwave, covered, on High for 1 to 2 minutes or until cheese melts. Let stand, covered, for 3 minutes before serving.

Micro-Tips

To microwave shredded cabbage: Place 4 cups (1 L) shredded cabbage in an 8-cup (2 L) baking dish with ⅓ cup (75 mL) water. Microwave, covered, on High for 5 to 8 minutes, stirring once, until tender-crisp.

To cook cabbage wedges: Cut ½ medium cabbage into 1½-inch (4 cm) thick wedges. Place thicker edges toward outside of 10-cup (2.5 L) shallow rectangular baking dish, with thinner edges toward center of dish. Add ⅓ cup (75 mL) water and cover with plastic wrap with one corner turned back to vent. Microwave on High for 8 to 12 minutes or until just tender.

Sauerkraut with Knackwurst and Apples

Supermarket deli counters stock an array of smoked and cooked sausages for easy-to-prepare meals. Any combination of cooked sausages can be used in this recipe. Serve this hearty dish with a selection of mustards and boiled potatoes.

Tip

Cooked smoked sausages, such as debreczner, thick slices of kielbasa or cubed cooked ham can be substituted for the knackwurst. For whole sausages, pierce their skins using a skewer to prevent skins from bursting, or cut into large chunks and add to dish.

8- or 12-cup (2 to 3 L) casserole dish with lid

1 tbsp	butter	15 mL
1	onion, chopped	1
1	can (28 oz/796 mL) sauerkraut, rinsed and squeezed dry	1
2	apples, cored and chopped	2
¾ cup	apple cider or juice	175 mL
2 tbsp	packed brown sugar	25 mL
1 tbsp	Dijon mustard	15 mL
	Freshly ground black pepper	
1 lb	knackwurst (see Tip, left)	500 g

1. In casserole dish, combine butter and onion. Microwave, covered, on High for 2 to 3 minutes or until onion is softened. Stir in sauerkraut and apples.

2. In a small bowl, combine apple cider, brown sugar and mustard. Pour over sauerkraut. Season with pepper to taste. Microwave, covered, on High for 12 to 18 minutes, stirring once, until mixture is tender.

3. Pierce skins of knackwurst in several places with a wooden skewer or toothpick and partially bury in sauerkraut. Microwave, covered, on Medium (50%) for 5 to 8 minutes or until heated through. Let stand, covered, for 5 minutes.

Micro-Tip

Sausages, such as debreczner (a smoked cooked sausage), knackwurst, Hungarian and wieners, can be easily steamed in the microwave oven. Before cooking, pierce their skins using a skewer or toothpick in several places to prevent them from bursting when heated. Place 1 lb (500 g) sausages in a covered casserole with ¼ cup (50 mL) water. Microwave on Medium (50%), rearranging once, for 5 to 8 minutes or until heated through.

Sausage, Corn and Black Bean Chili

Use your microwave to beat the cold with an appealing one-dish meal that takes just 30 minutes to prepare.

Tips

Any kind of canned beans such as chickpeas or Romano beans can be used. Canned beans and salsa tend to be on the salty side, so there is no need to add additional salt.

Instead of sausage meat, cook whole sausages in a large nonstick skillet on the stovetop or grill on the barbecue until no longer pink inside and juices run clear. Another suggestion is to cook extra sausages when barbecuing and use the next night in this pleasing chili. Cut the cooked sausages into slices and add to dish along with salsa and beans.

8-cup (2 L) casserole dish with lid

12 oz	hot or mild Italian sausages	375 g
1	onion, chopped	1
2	cloves garlic, minced	2
1	large green bell pepper, chopped	1
1 tbsp	chili powder or more to taste	15 mL
1½ cups	mild or medium salsa	375 mL
1	can (7½ oz/213 mL) tomato sauce	1
1	can (19 oz/540 mL) black beans, drained and rinsed (see Tips, left)	1
1 cup	frozen corn kernels	250 mL
⅓ cup	beef stock or water	75 mL
1 cup	shredded Cheddar cheese	250 mL
¼ cup	chopped fresh cilantro (optional)	50 mL

1. Remove skins of sausages and crumble meat into casserole dish. Cover with waxed paper. Microwave on High for 5 to 7 minutes, until sausage is no longer pink, stirring twice with a fork to break up meat lumps. Drain off any excess fat in dish.

2. Add onion, garlic, green pepper and chili powder to dish. Microwave, covered, on High for 4 to 6 minutes or until vegetables are tender.

3. Add salsa, tomato sauce, beans, corn and stock. Microwave, covered, on High for 7 to 11 minutes, stirring once, until piping hot and corn is tender.

4. Ladle into bowls and top with cheese and cilantro, if using.

Micro-Tip

One of the best advantages of microwaving a stew or one-pot meal is that it comes to the table in the microwave casserole so there's less cleanup than stovetop or oven-baked dishes.

Lamb Stew with Apricots

This Indian-style stew is especially good served with couscous or basmati rice.

8-cup (2 L) casserole dish with lid

1 tbsp	vegetable oil	15 mL
1	onion, chopped	1
2	cloves garlic, minced	2
2 tsp	mild curry paste or powder	10 mL
1 lb	stewing lamb or pork, cut into ¾-inch (2 cm) cubes	500 g
1 tbsp	all-purpose flour	15 mL
1	apple, peeled and diced	1
⅓ cup	chopped dried apricots	75 mL
¾ cup	chicken stock	175 mL
2 tbsp	soy sauce	25 mL
2 tbsp	mango chutney	25 mL
¼ cup	chopped fresh cilantro	50 mL
	Salt (optional)	

1. In casserole dish, combine oil, onion, garlic and curry paste. Microwave, covered, on High for 2 to 3 minutes or until softened.

2. In a bowl, toss lamb with flour. Add to casserole dish with apple, apricots, stock, soy sauce and mango chutney. Microwave, covered, on High for 5 to 7 minutes or until mixture comes to a boil.

3. Microwave on Medium (50%) for 18 to 24 minutes longer, stirring once, until meat is tender. Sprinkle with cilantro. Season with salt to taste, if desired. Let stand, covered, for 5 minutes before serving.

Fish and Seafood

Shrimp in Red Pepper Cream Sauce

Serves 4

I like to serve this richly flavored sauce, which features convenient frozen shrimp, over rice or noodles.

8-cup (2 L) casserole dish with lid

2 tbsp	butter	25 mL
4	green onions, sliced	4
1	large red bell pepper, diced	1
3 tbsp	all-purpose flour	45 mL
½ cup	fish or chicken stock (approx.)	125 mL
½ cup	whipping (35%) cream	125 mL
¼ cup	white wine or additional stock	50 mL
½ tsp	salt	2 mL
	Ground white pepper	
1	package (14 oz/400 g) frozen cooked medium shrimp, peeled	1
2 tbsp	chopped fresh dill, parsley or basil	25 mL

1. In casserole dish, combine butter, onions and red pepper. Microwave, covered, on High for 3 to 4 minutes or until softened.

2. In a bowl, blend flour with stock until smooth. Stir into casserole along with cream, wine, salt, and pepper to taste. Microwave, uncovered, on High for 3½ to 5 minutes, stirring once, until sauces boils and thickens. (Sauce will be thick.)

3. Add frozen shrimp. Microwave, covered, on Medium (50%) for 3 to 5 minutes, stirring once, until piping hot. (Do not overcook shrimp; they should be defrosted and heated through.) Sprinkle with dill and serve.

Cod with Spicy Tomato Sauce

Serves 3 to 4

Fish has a natural affinity for the microwave. It comes out moist and tender and cooks in a matter of minutes. Serve with boiled potatoes or rice along with a green salad.

8-inch (2 L) square baking dish or 11-by 7-inch (2 L) baking dish
4-cup (1 L) casserole dish with lid

1	package (14 oz/400 g) frozen cod fillets, flounder or perch (see Micro-Tip, below)	1
1 tbsp	olive oil	15 mL
1	small onion, halved lengthwise, thinly sliced	1
1	clove garlic, minced	1
½	yellow or red bell pepper, chopped	½
¼ tsp	hot pepper flakes	1 mL
1 cup	well-drained chopped canned tomatoes	250 mL
	Salt and freshly ground black pepper	
10	dry-cured black olives	10
1 tbsp	capers, rinsed and drained	15 mL
2 tbsp	chopped fresh parsley	25 mL

1. Remove fish from wrapping and place in baking dish. Microwave, uncovered, on High for 2 to 4 minutes or until defrosted enough that fish can be cut into 3 or 4 serving pieces. Drain off any liquid in dish. Set fish aside.

2. In 4-cup (1 L) casserole dish, combine oil, onion, garlic, yellow pepper and hot pepper flakes. Microwave, covered, on High for 2 to 3 minutes or until softened.

3. Add tomatoes. Season with salt and pepper to taste. Microwave, covered, on High for 3 to 5 minutes or until sauce-like. Add olives, capers and parsley.

4. Spoon tomato sauce over cod. Cover with plastic wrap and turn back one corner to vent. Microwave, covered, on High for 6 to 9 minutes or until fish is opaque. Let stand, covered, for 3 minutes before serving.

Micro-Tip

If using fresh fish fillets, pour sauce over fish and cook, covered, on Medium-High (70%) for 4 to 7 minutes or until fish is opaque.

Salmon with Creamy Tomato Dill Sauce

Looking for entertaining ways to serve salmon? Fresh salmon is readily available at most supermarkets and makes for a special spring dinner with small new potatoes and asparagus.

4-cup (1 L) casserole dish
10-cup (2.5 L) shallow rectangular baking dish or 11-by 7-inch (2 L) baking dish

1 tbsp	butter	15 mL
1/4 cup	finely chopped shallots	50 mL
1	clove garlic, finely minced	1
1	large ripe tomato, seeded and diced	1
1 tsp	cornstarch	5 mL
1/4 cup	whipping (35%) cream	50 mL
2 tbsp	chopped fresh dill	25 mL
4	salmon fillets (each 5 oz/150 g), skins removed (see Micro-Tip, below)	4
1/3 cup	white wine or stock	75 mL
	Salt and freshly ground black pepper	

1. In casserole dish, combine butter, shallots and garlic. Microwave, covered, on High for 2 minutes to soften. Add tomato. Microwave, covered, on High for 2 to 3 minutes or until tomato is sauce-like.

2. In a small bowl, blend cornstarch with 1 tsp (5 mL) cold water. Stir into casserole dish along with cream and dill. Set aside.

3. Arrange salmon in baking dish. Pour wine over top. Cover with plastic wrap and turn back one corner to vent. Microwave on Medium (50%) for 4 to 7 minutes or until fish is opaque. Drain liquid from dish into tomato mixture. Season with salt and pepper to taste. Keep salmon covered while finishing sauce.

4. Microwave sauce, uncovered, on High for 2 to 3 minutes, stirring once, until it comes to a boil and thickens slightly. Place salmon fillets on serving plates and spoon sauce over top.

Micro-Tip

Salmon cooks very quickly in the microwave oven. It has a higher fat content than white fish, such as sole, and tends to sputter and pop when microwaved on High. As a general guideline, cook salmon on Medium (50%) to overcome the problem. Cooking time will also depend on the thickness of the salmon, so always undercook slightly since it continues to cook after it comes out of the microwave.

Sole with Orange Ginger Sauce

Serves 4

■ Fish and the microwave oven were meant for each other. Fish cooks so quickly and stays so moist thanks to the steam-like cooking method of the microwave.

Tip

I like to double this superb sweet-sour orange sauce and have it handy in the fridge to use as a quick baste when grilling chicken or pork. It also makes a great warm dipping sauce for chicken nuggets or fish sticks. Store sauce in a covered container in the refrigerator for up to 1 week.

8-inch (2 L) square baking dish or 11-by 7-inch (2 L) baking dish

ORANGE GINGER SAUCE

½ cup	orange juice	125 mL
1 tbsp	soy sauce	15 mL
1 tbsp	rice vinegar	15 mL
2 tsp	packed brown sugar	10 mL
1½ tsp	cornstarch	7 mL
1 tsp	minced fresh gingerroot	5 mL
1 lb	sole, haddock or cod fillets	500 g
2	green onions, sliced	2

1. In a glass measure, stir together orange juice, soy sauce, vinegar, brown sugar, cornstarch and ginger until smooth. Microwave, uncovered, on High for 1 to 1½ minutes, stirring once, until sauce comes to a full boil and thickens. (Sauce will be quite thick.)

2. Pat fish fillets dry with paper towels. Arrange in a single layer in baking dish. For thin fillets, such as sole, turn tapered ends under. Spread with sauce. Sprinkle with green onions. Cover with plastic wrap and turn back one corner to vent. Microwave on Medium-High (70%) for 3½ to 5 minutes or until fish is opaque. Let stand, covered, for 2 minutes before serving.

Mediterranean Sole with Potatoes

The microwave oven has been a great boon to frozen fish. We no longer need to remember hours ahead of time to defrost the fish fillets in the refrigerator. Here, I've taken sole directly from the freezer to defrost in the microwave, then added some white wine, black olives and other Mediterranean delights for a surprisingly easy one-dish wonder.

Variation

You can substitute other fresh or frozen fish fillets, such as snapper, tilapia, cod or catfish for the sole.

9-inch (23 cm) microwave-safe deep pie plate

1	package (10 oz/300 g) individually frozen sole fillets	1
3/4 cup	finely sliced leeks, white and light green part only	175 mL
1 cup	sliced mushrooms	250 mL
2	potatoes, peeled and very thinly sliced	2
1/4 cup	white wine, or chicken or fish stock	50 mL
Pinch	saffron threads, crushed (optional)	Pinch
1/4 tsp	salt	1 mL
	Freshly ground black pepper	
2 tbsp	chopped drained oil-packed or rehydrated sun-dried tomatoes (see Micro-Tip, right)	25 mL
2 tbsp	chopped black olives, such as Kalamata	25 mL
2 tbsp	chopped fresh parsley	25 mL
2 tsp	capers, rinsed and drained	10 mL
1 tbsp	olive oil	15 mL

1. Remove fish from wrapping, separate fillets and place on a plate. Microwave, uncovered, on Defrost (30%) for 3 to 4 minutes or until a few ice crystals remain in fish. Let drain on paper towels until completely defrosted.

2. Place leeks and mushrooms in baking dish. Top with potatoes in an even layer.

3. In a glass measure, combine wine with saffron, if using. Season with salt, and pepper to taste. Pour over potatoes. Cover with lid or plastic wrap with one corner turned back to vent.

4. Microwave on High for 4 to 6 minutes or until potatoes are just tender when tested with a fork.

5. Top with fish fillets in an even layer. Sprinkle with sun-dried tomatoes, olives, parsley and capers. Drizzle with oil. Microwave, covered, on High for 3 to 5 minutes or until fish is opaque. Let stand, covered, for 2 minutes before serving.

Micro-Tip

Use oil-packed or reconstituted sun-dried tomatoes. To rehydrate sun-dried tomatoes: Place 1 cup (250 mL) hot tap water in 2 cup (500 mL) glass measure. Add 1/2 cup (125 mL) dried tomato halves. Microwave, uncovered, on High for 2 to 3 minutes or until boiling. Let stand for 5 minutes or until softened. Drain and pat dry. Store rehydrated tomatoes in a covered container in the refrigerator for up to 1 week or freeze.

Halibut with Cucumber Sauce

This simple yet special dish features halibut or salmon. Dressed with a cucumber and dill sauce, it wouldn't be out of place at your next elegant dinner party.

10-cup (2.5 L) shallow rectangular baking dish or 11-by 7-inch (2 L) baking dish
4-cup (1 L) glass measure

1¼ lbs	halibut or salmon steaks	625 g
⅓ cup	white wine	75 mL

CUCUMBER DILL SAUCE

2 tsp	cornstarch	10 mL
2	green onions, sliced	2
⅓ cup	sour cream (regular or light)	75 mL
¾ cup	finely diced peeled English cucumber	175 mL
2 tbsp	finely chopped fresh dill or parsley	25 mL
½ tsp	salt	2 mL
	Freshly ground black pepper	

1. Arrange halibut in single layer in baking dish. Pour wine over top. Cover with plastic wrap and turn back one corner to vent. Microwave on High for 4 to 6 minutes or until fish just turns opaque.

2. Turn back one corner of plastic wrap and place a plate over fish to hold in place. Carefully pour juices into glass measure. Keep fish covered while preparing sauce.

3. *Cucumber Dill Sauce:* In a small bowl, blend cornstarch with 2 tsp (10 mL) cold water. Stir into reserved fish juices along with green onions. Microwave sauce, uncovered, on High for 1½ to 2½ minutes, stirring once, until sauce comes to a full boil and thickens.

4. Add sour cream, cucumber and dill. Season with salt, and pepper to taste.

5. Microwave sauce, uncovered, on High for 1 to 2 minutes or until just heated through. Pour over halibut to serve.

Micro-Tips

Fresh fish cooks very quickly in the microwave oven. Allow 3½ to 5 minutes per lb or 8 to 11 minutes per kg and undercook slightly since fish will continue to cook on standing time.

For even cooking, always arrange the thicker portion of fish fillet or steaks to the outside of the dish and thinner tapered edges toward the center.

Trout with Fresh Tomato Herb Sauce

■ Here's a summery no-fuss cooking technique for trout or salmon or any of your favorite fish, including red snapper or tilapia. Serve with new baby potatoes and green beans.

Tip

Use extra virgin olive oil and vine-ripened tomatoes for maximum flavor.

10-cup (2.5 L) shallow rectangular baking dish or 11-by 7-inch (2 L) baking dish

2	ripe tomatoes, seeded and diced	2
2 tbsp	chopped fresh basil or chives	25 mL
2 tbsp	chopped fresh parsley	25 mL
1 tbsp	balsamic vinegar	15 mL
2 tbsp	olive oil, divided	25 mL
	Salt and freshly ground black pepper	
4	trout fillets (each 5 oz/150 g)	4
1/4 cup	white wine or chicken stock	50 mL

1. In a bowl, combine tomatoes, basil, parsley, vinegar and 1 tbsp (15 mL) of the oil. Season with salt and pepper to taste. Set aside.

2. Place trout in baking dish. Season fillets with salt and pepper. Drizzle with remaining olive oil and wine.

3. Cover with plastic wrap and turn back one corner to vent. Microwave on Medium (50%) for $3\frac{1}{2}$ to 5 minutes or until fish is opaque. Let stand, covered, for 2 minutes. To serve, arrange fish on serving plates and top with a spoonful of the tomato sauce.

Spanish Fish Stew

I love this zesty Mediterranean fish stew that calls for saffron, which lends a brilliant orange color and distinctive flavor to fish and potatoes. For an easy supper fit for company, just add crusty bread and a salad of baby greens as a starter.

Tip
Add ¼ tsp (1 mL) hot pepper flakes if you like a touch of heat in this robust fish stew.

8-cup (2 L) casserole dish with lid

1	package (14 oz/400 g) frozen fish fillets, such as haddock or cod	1
2 tbsp	olive oil	25 mL
1	large onion, chopped	1
1	large garlic clove, minced	1
2 cups	cubed peeled potatoes	500 mL
¼ tsp	crushed saffron threads	1 mL
¼ tsp	dried thyme leaves	1 mL
1	small bay leaf	1
1	yellow or red bell pepper, diced	1
1	can (19 oz/540 mL) tomatoes, including juice, chopped	1
½ tsp	salt	2 mL
	Freshly ground black pepper	
2 tbsp	chopped fresh parsley	25 mL

1. Remove fish from wrapping and place on a large plate. Microwave, uncovered, on High for 3 to 5 minutes, rearranging once, until partly thawed. Cut fish into ³⁄₄-inch (2 cm) cubes and set aside.

2. In casserole dish, combine oil, onion, garlic, potatoes, saffron, thyme and bay leaf. Microwave, covered, on High for 6 to 9 minutes, stirring once, until potatoes are almost tender.

3. Add yellow pepper, tomatoes, salt, and pepper to taste. Microwave, covered, on High for 7 to 10 minutes or until potatoes are tender.

4. Stir in fish and parsley. Microwave, covered, on High for 2 to 3 minutes or until fish is opaque. Let stand, covered, for 3 minutes. Remove bay leaf before serving.

Salmon with Creamy Tomato Dill Sauce (page 90)

Overleaf: Curried Lentil Stew with Vegetables (page 116)

Pasta, Grains and Legumes

Trout with Fresh Tomato
Herb Sauce (page 95)

Beefy Macaroni and Zucchini Casserole

Serves 4 to 6

■ Get a head start on dinner by preparing this family-favorite dish the night before. Just pop the casserole in the microwave as you come through the door for a superfast meal that is ready in 20 minutes.

Tip

There is a large assortment of bottled pasta sauces available with different herb and flavor combinations. Choose whatever sauce appeals to you for this recipe.

Instead of zucchini, add 1½ cups (375 mL) fresh, canned or frozen corn kernels or peas to pasta mixture.

8-cup (2 L) casserole dish with lid

QUICK SPAGHETTI SAUCE

1 lb	lean ground beef	500 g
1	onion, chopped	1
2	cloves garlic, minced	2
1 tsp	dried basil leaves	5 mL
1 tsp	dried oregano leaves	5 mL
½ tsp	salt	2 mL
	Freshly ground black pepper	
1	jar (25 oz/700 mL) tomato pasta sauce	1
2 cups	elbow macaroni	500 mL
2	zucchini, thinly sliced, divided	2
1 cup	shredded provolone or mozzarella cheese	250 mL

1. *Quick Spaghetti Sauce:* Crumble beef into casserole dish and microwave, uncovered, on High for 5 to 7 minutes, until beef is no longer pink, stirring twice with a fork to break up meat lumps. Drain off any excess fat in dish.

2. Add onion, garlic, basil, oregano, salt and pepper to dish. Microwave, covered, on High, for 3 to 5 minutes, stirring once, until onion is tender. Stir in tomato pasta sauce. Microwave, covered, on High for 8 to 12 minutes or until flavors are blended.

3. In a large pot of boiling salted water, cook pasta until just tender but firm, about 8 minutes. Drain and return to pot. Stir in Quick Spaghetti Sauce and toss well.

4. Layer one-third of the pasta mixture in casserole dish. Cover with half of the sliced zucchini. Repeat with another layer of pasta and zucchini. Top with remaining pasta. (Can be prepared a day ahead and refrigerated.)

5. Microwave, covered, on High for 12 to 16 minutes (add 5 minutes longer if refrigerated) or until zucchini is tender. Sprinkle with cheese. Microwave, uncovered, on High for 1 to 2 minutes or until cheese is melted. Let stand, covered, for 5 minutes.

Spicy Spaghettini with Peppers and Olives

Serves 4 as a main course, 6 to 8 as a side dish

A jar of roasted red peppers, along with a few other kitchen staples, forms the base of this simple pasta dish packed with bold flavors. I like to serve it with a salad of mixed bitter greens, such as radicchio, endive and leaf lettuce. The pasta also teams well with grilled sausages.

8-cup (2 L) casserole dish with lid

1	jar (13 oz/370 g) roasted red peppers	1
12 oz	spaghettini	375 g
½ cup	dry-cured small black olives	125 mL
2 tbsp	capers, rinsed and drained	25 mL
3 tbsp	olive oil	45 mL
1	small red onion, chopped	1
3	large cloves garlic, minced	3
1½ tsp	dried oregano leaves	7 mL
¼ tsp	hot pepper flakes or more to taste	1 mL
½ cup	chopped fresh parsley	125 mL
¾ cup	freshly grated Romano cheese	175 mL
	Salt and freshly ground black pepper	

1. Drain roasted peppers. Rinse and pat dry. Cut into 2-inch (5 cm) strips.

2. In a large pot of boiling salted water, cook pasta until tender but still firm, about 5 to 7 minutes. Reserve ⅓ cup (75 mL) of cooking liquid. Drain pasta well and return to pot.

3. Meanwhile in casserole dish, combine red peppers, olives, capers, oil, onion, garlic, oregano and hot pepper flakes. Microwave, covered, on High for 3 to 5 minutes or until onion is tender. Add to drained hot pasta along with reserved cooking liquid, parsley and Romano cheese. Toss well. Season with salt and pepper to taste. Serve immediately.

Micro-Tip

I often cook additional pasta to have on hand to serve as a side dish sprinkled with Parmesan. To reheat, place cooked pasta in casserole dish and add 1 tbsp (15 mL) water or chicken stock per cup (250 mL) of cooked pasta. (The added moisture creates steam to prevent pasta from drying out.) Microwave, covered, on High for about 1 minute per cup (250 mL) of pasta (or use the sensor reheat feature of your microwave oven). Toss with desired amount of butter or drizzle with olive oil and sprinkle with freshly grated Parmesan cheese.

Creamy Tortellini with Basil and Walnut Sauce

Serves 2 as a main course, 3 to 4 as a starter

Use Californian walnuts for best flavor in this time-saving pasta sauce that you set in the microwave while cooking the pasta on the stovetop.

8-cup (2 L) glass measure

½ cup	whipping (35%) cream	125 mL
½ cup	chicken stock	125 mL
3	green onions, sliced	3
2	cloves garlic, minced	2
½ cup	finely chopped walnuts	125 mL
12 oz	cheese- or meat-stuffed tortellini	375 g
⅓ cup	lightly packed fresh basil, chopped	75 mL
⅓ cup	freshly grated Parmesan cheese	75 mL
	Salt and freshly ground black pepper	

1. In glass measure, combine cream, stock, green onions, garlic and walnuts. Microwave, uncovered, on High for 4 to 7 minutes, stirring once, until sauce comes to a full rolling boil and thickens slightly.

2. Meanwhile, in large pot of boiling salted water, cook pasta until tender but firm, according to package directions. Drain well. Add to cream mixture along with basil and Parmesan cheese. Toss well. Season with salt and pepper to taste. Serve immediately.

Micro-Tip

When to cover or not cover a dish in the microwave? Covering a dish will allow foods to cook faster and helps retain moisture. Uncover a dish when you want to evaporate some of the moisture so that liquid will reduce and thicken a sauce.

Tuna Mushroom Bake

Serves 4

A tasty tuna casserole is an indispensable part of today's comfort kitchen — satisfying and ever so simple to make. I often make the sauce ahead and refrigerate or freeze it, then toss it with the hot cooked pasta when I need dinner ready in a hurry.

8-cup (2 L) casserole dish with lid

1 tbsp	butter	15 mL
4	green onions, sliced	4
2 cups	sliced mushrooms (6 oz/175 g)	500 mL
2 tbsp	all-purpose flour	25 mL
1 cup	chicken stock, divided	250 mL
1/2 cup	half-and-half (10%) cream or milk	125 mL
1	can (6 1/2 oz/170 g) water-packed tuna, drained and flaked	1
1/3 cup	freshly grated Parmesan cheese	75 mL
1 1/2 cups	elbow macaroni	375 mL
	Salt and freshly ground black pepper	

1. In casserole dish, combine butter, green onions and mushrooms. Microwave, covered, on High for 4 to 6 minutes, stirring once, until vegetables are tender.

2. In a bowl, blend flour with 1/3 cup (75 mL) of the stock until smooth. Stir into mushroom mixture along with remaining stock and cream. Microwave, uncovered, on High for 4 to 6 minutes, stirring once, until sauce boils and thickens. Stir in tuna and Parmesan cheese.

3. Meanwhile, in a large pot of boiling salted water, cook pasta until tender but firm, about 8 minutes. Drain well. Stir pasta into sauce. Season with salt and pepper to taste.

4. Microwave, covered, on High for 2 to 3 minutes, stirring once, until piping hot. Serve immediately.

Quick Vegetable Lasagna

Serves 6

Nothing beats the taste of old-fashioned lasagna made with long-simmered tomato sauce, but in a pinch, this shortcut version is a great stand-in. To save time, buy oven-ready lasagna noodles available in supermarkets or cook regular lasagna noodles.

8-cup (2 L) casserole dish with lid
10-cup (2.5 L) shallow rectangular baking dish
(see Micro-Tips, right)

1 tbsp	olive oil	15 mL
1	red or green bell pepper, chopped	1
1	zucchini, halved lengthwise and sliced	1
2 cups	sliced mushrooms (6 oz/175 g)	500 mL
1 tsp	dried basil leaves	5 mL
1	jar (25 oz/700 mL) tomato pasta sauce with sun-dried tomatoes	1
1	egg	1
1 cup	ricotta cheese	250 mL
1/4 cup	freshly grated Parmesan cheese	50 mL
	Salt and freshly ground black pepper	
9	oven-ready lasagna noodles	9
1 1/2 cups	shredded Friulano, Fontina or mozzarella cheese	375 mL

1. In casserole dish, combine oil, red pepper, zucchini, mushrooms and basil. Microwave, covered, on High for 4 to 6 minutes, stirring once, until vegetables are just tender. Stir in tomato pasta sauce.

2. In a bowl, beat egg. Stir in ricotta and Parmesan cheeses. Season with salt and pepper to taste.

3. Spoon some of the sauce in bottom of baking dish to form a thin layer. Layer 3 lasagna noodles over top. Spread one-third of the remaining sauce over noodles. Cover with 3 more lasagna noodles. Spread with another one-third of the sauce. Spread ricotta filling over top. Cover with remaining noodles and top with remaining sauce. Cover with plastic wrap and turn back one corner to vent.

4. Microwave on High for 5 minutes. Reduce to Medium (50%) and microwave for 12 to 16 minutes or until center is hot and noodles are just tender.

5. Sprinkle with cheese and microwave, uncovered, on High for 1 to 2 minutes or until melted. Let stand for 10 minutes before cutting into squares.

Micro-Tips

■ Always test to ensure that the dish you are using fits in your microwave oven before preparing the recipe. If the dish that is called for, such as the 10-cup (2.5 L) baking dish recommended in this recipe, is too large for your microwave oven, you may opt to prepare the recipe in 2 smaller baking dishes and cook them one at a time. Reduce microwave cooking times by about one-third for each casserole dish.

■ If you have a built-in turntable and the casserole does not turn because of its size, rotate the dish several times during cooking to promote even cooking.

Chicken Penne Casserole with Broccoli

Everyone enjoys this terrific homespun supper dish. It's a great way to take care of leftover roast chicken, turkey or ham after the holidays.

Tip

The sauce can be made a day ahead and refrigerated, but cook the pasta and assemble the casserole shortly before serving to prevent the pasta from absorbing all of the sauce.

8-cup (2 L) casserole dish with lid

1 tbsp	butter	15 mL
1	small onion, chopped	1
1	clove garlic, minced	1
2 cups	sliced mushrooms (6 oz/175 g)	500 mL
¾ tsp	dried Italian seasoning	4 mL
2 tbsp	all-purpose flour	25 mL
1⅓ cups	chicken stock, divided	325 mL
2 cups	diced cooked chicken, turkey or ham	500 mL
½ cup	sour cream (regular or light)	125 mL
	Salt and freshly ground black pepper	
2 cups	penne or other tube-shaped pasta	500 mL
4 cups	broccoli florets and trimmed stalks cut into small pieces	1 L
1 cup	shredded Cheddar or Fontina cheese	250 mL

1. In casserole dish, combine butter, onion, garlic, mushrooms and Italian seasoning. Microwave, covered, on High for 3 to 5 minutes, stirring once, until vegetables are softened.

2. In a bowl, blend flour with ⅓ cup (75 mL) of the stock until smooth. Stir into mushroom mixture along with remaining stock. Microwave, covered, on High for 3 to 5 minutes, stirring once, until sauce comes to a boil and thickens. Stir in chicken and sour cream. (Sauce can be made a day ahead, covered and refrigerated.)

3. Meanwhile, in a large pot of boiling salted water, cook pasta until almost tender, about 8 minutes. Add broccoli and return to boil. Cook for 1 minute longer, until broccoli is bright green and pasta is tender but firm. Drain well. Return to pot and add chicken mixture. Toss well. Season with salt and pepper to taste.

4. Transfer to casserole dish. Microwave, covered, on High for 4 to 6 minutes or until piping hot in center. (Microwave for 5 minutes longer if made ahead and refrigerated.)

5. Sprinkle with cheese and microwave, uncovered, on High for 1 to 2 minutes, or until melted.

Fusilli with Ricotta and Spinach

Serves 4

▨ Looking for a simple dish when you walk through the door at night? Count on this pasta dish, a favorite in my kitchen. There's little to chop and the sauce can be made a day or two ahead, so only the pasta needs to be cooked.

Tip

Sauce can be prepared 1 to 2 days ahead. Cover and refrigerate. Allow slightly longer microwave times to reheat sauce.

8-cup (2 L) casserole dish with lid

1	package (10 oz/300 g) frozen chopped spinach	1
1 tbsp	butter	15 mL
4	green onions, sliced	4
1 cup	ricotta cheese	250 mL
4 oz	herb and garlic cream cheese spread	125 g
1/2 cup	freshly grated Parmesan cheese	125 mL
3/4 cup	chicken stock	175 mL
1/4 tsp	freshly grated nutmeg	1 mL
	Salt and freshly ground black pepper	
4 cups	fusilli or penne pasta	1 L

1. Place spinach in casserole dish. Microwave, covered, on High for 4 to 6 minutes, stirring once, until defrosted and piping hot. Place in a strainer. Using the back of a spoon, squeeze out as much moisture as possible.

2. Return to casserole dish. Add butter and green onions. Microwave, covered, on High for 3 to 5 minutes, stirring once, until spinach is tender.

3. In a food processor or blender, purée ricotta, cream cheese, Parmesan, stock and nutmeg. Stir into spinach mixture.

4. Microwave sauce, uncovered, on High for 2 to 4 minutes or until piping hot. Season with salt and pepper to taste.

5. Meanwhile, in a large pot of boiling salted water, cook pasta until tender but firm, 8 to 10 minutes. Drain well. Add to spinach mixture and toss well. Serve immediately.

Linguine with Shrimp, Asparagus and Mushrooms

Fresh thyme, whether snipped from your garden or purchased from produce markets, lends a robust flavor to linguine along with earthy mushrooms and shrimp accented with lemon zest.

Tip

Never add oil to water when boiling pasta as it prevents the sauce from clinging to pasta when tossed.

4-cup (1 L) casserole dish with lid
8-cup (2 L) glass measure

1 lb	large cooked frozen shrimp, peeled with tails left on	500 g
1 tbsp	butter	15 mL
3 cups	sliced cremini mushrooms (about 9 oz/275 g)	750 mL
1	onion, chopped	1
2	large cloves garlic, minced	2
1 tbsp	chopped fresh thyme	15 mL
1 cup	whipping (35 %) cream	250 mL
1 tbsp	grated lemon zest	15 mL
1 tsp	salt	5 mL
	Freshly ground black pepper	
12 oz	linguine	375 g
1 lb	fresh asparagus, ends trimmed, cut into 1½-inch (4 cm) diagonal pieces	500 g
½ cup	freshly grated Parmesan cheese	125 mL
⅓ cup	chopped fresh parsley	75 mL

1. Place shrimp in casserole dish. Microwave, covered, on Medium (50%) for 4 to 6 minutes, stirring twice, until just defrosted. Drain in a sieve. Pat dry with paper towels to absorb excess moisture. Set aside.

2. In glass measure, combine butter, mushrooms, onion, garlic and thyme. Microwave, uncovered, on High for 4 to 6 minutes, stirring once, until mushrooms are softened.

3. Add cream, lemon zest and salt, and pepper to taste. Microwave, uncovered, on High for 4 to 7 minutes or until sauce boils and is slightly reduced. (Sauce can be prepared earlier on in day, covered and refrigerated. When ready to serve, microwave on High until sauce boils.)

4. Add shrimp and microwave, uncovered, on High for 1 minute or until just piping hot. Do not overcook or shrimp will toughen.

5. Meanwhile, in a large pot of boiling salted water, cook pasta until almost tender, about 5 to 7 minutes. Add asparagus and return water to a boil. Cook for 1 minute longer or until asparagus is bright green and crisp and pasta is tender but firm. Drain well and return to pot. Pour shrimp sauce over and toss. Stir in Parmesan cheese and parsley. Adjust seasoning with salt and pepper to taste. Toss again and serve immediately.

Micro-Tip

The microwave's short cooking time means that dried herbs often do not have a chance to fully impart their flavor in cooking. Substitute fresh for dried in your favorite recipes, if you have fresh herbs on hand. As a guideline, substitute 1 tbsp (15 mL) chopped fresh herbs for 1 tsp (5 mL) dried.

Homespun
Macaroni and Cheese

Serves 4

This '50s-style pasta dish never loses its homey appeal. Prepare the sauce in the microwave while cooking the pasta on the stovetop and you'll have dinner on the table in no time.

Tip

Casserole can also be baked conventionally. Prepare recipe to Step 4. Top with crumb topping but instead of placing under broiler, bake in preheated 350°F (180°C) oven for 20 to 25 minutes (add 15 minutes if made ahead and refrigerated).

8-cup (2 L) glass measure
8-cup (2 L) casserole dish (optional)

3 tbsp	butter	45 mL
1/4 cup	all-purpose flour	50 mL
1 tsp	dry mustard	5 mL
3 cups	milk	750 mL
2 cups	shredded aged Cheddar cheese	500 mL
1/2 tsp	salt	2 mL
Pinch	cayenne pepper	Pinch
2 1/2 cups	elbow macaroni	675 mL

CRUMB TOPPING (OPTIONAL)

1 tbsp	butter	15 mL
3/4 cup	soft fresh bread crumbs (1 slice bread)	175 mL
1/4 cup	freshly grated Parmesan cheese	50 mL

1. Place butter in a small bowl and microwave, uncovered, on High for 40 to 60 seconds or until melted and bubbling. Stir in flour and mustard to make a paste.

2. In glass measure, microwave milk, uncovered, on High for 5 to 7 minutes or until piping hot. Whisk in flour mixture until smooth. Microwave, uncovered, on High for 2 to 3 minutes, stirring once, until mixture comes to a full boil and thickens. (Watch carefully to prevent mixture from boiling over.) Stir in cheese until melted. Season with salt and cayenne pepper.

3. Meanwhile, in a large pot of boiling salted water, cook pasta just until tender but firm, about 8 minutes. Drain well and toss with cheese sauce until well coated. (Serve immediately or prepare with crumb topping, if using.)

4. *Crumb Topping:* Preheat broiler. Place pasta in casserole dish. In a glass bowl, melt butter, uncovered, on High for 15 to 30 seconds. Toss with bread crumbs and Parmesan cheese. Sprinkle over pasta. Place casserole under preheated broiler 4 inches (10 cm) from heat for about 3 minutes or until top is golden brown (watch carefully to prevent burning).

Micro-Tip

■ To make Homespun Macaroni and Cheese ahead: Place pasta in casserole dish, cover and refrigerate for up to 1 day ahead. Microwave, covered, on High for 9 to 13 minutes, stirring often, until piping hot. Smooth top and add crumb topping, if desired. Place under broiler as directed in recipe.

Make cheese sauce ahead, place in covered container and freeze. Transfer to a casserole dish or glass measure. Start on High, breaking up sauce until defrosted and sauce can be stirred. Reheat on Medium (50%) and microwave, stirring often, until piping hot.

Risotto with Parmesan

Rich and creamy risotto is far easier to make in the microwave oven as there's no need for all the stirring normally required when made on the stovetop. Once you try this easy microwave method, you'll never bother going back to cooking risotto the old-fashioned way on the stovetop.

Variation

Asparagus Risotto
Snap off woody ends of 1 lb (500 g) asparagus and peel if necessary. Cut on the diagonal into 1-inch (2.5 cm) pieces. Cook risotto as directed in recipe. Cover and let stand while cooking asparagus. Place asparagus in 4-cup (1 L) casserole dish with 1/4 cup (50 mL) chicken stock. Microwave, covered, on High for 4 to 6 minutes, stirring once during cooking, until tender-crisp. Stir asparagus, including cooking liquid, into rice along with Parmesan cheese and parsley. Season to taste with salt and pepper. Serve immediately.

4-cup (1 L) glass measure
8-cup (2 L) casserole dish with lid

2 cups	chicken stock (approx.)	500 mL
2 tbsp	butter	25 mL
1	small onion, finely chopped	1
1 cup	Arborio rice	250 mL
1/4 cup	dry white wine (or additional chicken stock)	50 mL
1/3 cup	freshly grated Parmesan cheese	75 mL
2 tbsp	chopped fresh parsley	25 mL
	Salt and freshly ground black pepper	

1. In glass measure, combine chicken stock and 1 cup (250 mL) water. Microwave, uncovered, on High for 5 to 8 minutes or until boiling. Set aside.

2. In casserole dish, combine butter and onion. Microwave, covered, on High for 2 minutes or until onion is softened. Add rice and stir to coat well. Stir in 2¾ cups (675 mL) of the reserved hot stock and wine.

3. Microwave, covered, on High for 3 to 5 minutes or until boiling. Reduce to Medium (50%) and microwave for 9 to 13 minutes, stirring once, until rice is just tender (rice should still be moist). Let stand, covered, for 5 minutes. Add more hot chicken stock, if necessary to achieve a moist creamy consistency. Stir in Parmesan and parsley. Season with salt, if needed, and pepper. Serve immediately.

Brown Rice Pilaf with Black Olives and Feta

■ Feta cheese and olives are salty, so be cautious about adding extra salt or using salty commercial stock bases. I like to increase the feta cheese to 1 cup (250 mL) and serve this flavorful rice dish as a main course along with a green salad.

8-cup (2 L) casserole dish with lid

1 tbsp	olive oil	15 mL
1	onion, chopped	1
1	large clove garlic, minced	1
1 tsp	dried oregano leaves	5 mL
1 cup	long-grain brown rice	250 mL
2½ cups	chicken or vegetable stock	625 mL
1	large red bell pepper, diced	1
½ cup	crumbled feta cheese	125 mL
¼ cup	chopped Kalamata olives	50 mL
¼ cup	chopped fresh parsley	50 mL
	Freshly ground black pepper	

1. In casserole dish, combine oil, onion, garlic and oregano. Microwave, covered, on High for 2 to 3 minutes to soften. Add rice and stock. Microwave, covered, on High for 5 to 8 minutes or until stock boils.

2. Reduce to Medium-Low (30%) and microwave for 18 to 20 minutes longer. Stir in red pepper and microwave, covered, on Medium-Low (30%) for 5 to 8 minutes or until most of the liquid is absorbed.

3. Stir in feta, olives and parsley. Season with pepper to taste. Let stand, covered, for 5 minutes.

Micro-Tip

■ To microwave brown rice: In 8-cup (2 L) casserole dish, combine 1 cup (250 mL) long-grain brown rice and 2½ cups (625 mL) stock or water. (If using water, add 1 tsp (5 mL) salt.) Microwave, covered, on High for 5 to 8 minutes or until boiling. Reduce to Medium-Low (30%) for 20 to 26 minutes or until most of the liquid has been absorbed. Let stand, covered, for 5 minutes. Makes 3 cups (750 mL).

Mushroom Rice Pilaf

Serves 4 to 6

■ While cooking rice in the microwave instead of on the stovetop isn't a great timesaver, I like the convenience of worry-free cooking and less cleanup when cooking and serving in one dish.

8-cup (2 L) casserole dish with lid

1 tbsp	butter	15 mL
1	small onion, chopped	1
1	clove garlic, minced	1
2 cups	sliced mushrooms (6 oz/175 g)	500 mL
½ tsp	dried thyme leaves	2 mL
1 cup	long-grain white rice	250 mL
1¾ cups	chicken stock	425 mL
2 tbsp	chopped fresh parsley	25 mL
	Salt and freshly ground black pepper	

1. In casserole dish, combine butter, onion, garlic, mushrooms and thyme. Microwave, covered, on High for 3 to 5 minutes or until mushrooms are tender.

2. Stir in rice and stock. Microwave, covered, on High for 4 to 6 minutes. Reduce to Medium (50%) and microwave for 10 to 14 minutes or until liquid is absorbed and rice is just tender.

3. Let stand, covered, for 10 minutes. Stir in parsley. Season with salt and pepper to taste.

Micro-Tips

■ Water and stock are the liquids most often used to cook rice, but you can add interest by using vegetable juice, lemon zest, wine, diced vegetables and herbs to add flavor.

■ How to reheat rice: Rice can be cooked ahead of time and reheated. Let cool, cover and refrigerate for up to 2 days. Add a small amount of additional moisture to steam rice when reheating — about 1 scant tbsp (15 mL) water per cup (250 mL) of packed cooked rice — and microwave, covered, on High until piping hot.

Potato and Chickpea Chili

Warm up on a cold, blustery night with this comforting vegetarian chili.

Variation

Add 1½ cups (375 mL) diced leftover roast lamb or ham along with the chickpeas for a meat lover's version of this hearty stew.

8-cup (2 L) casserole dish with lid

1 tbsp	olive oil	15 mL
2 cups	diced peeled potatoes, cut into ½-inch (1 cm) cubes	500 mL
1	onion, finely chopped	1
2	cloves garlic, minced	2
1 tbsp	chili powder or to taste	15 mL
1 tsp	ground cumin	5 mL
½ tsp	salt	2 mL
¼ tsp	hot pepper flakes (optional)	1 mL
1	can (19 oz/540 mL) stewed tomatoes, including juice, chopped	1
1	can (19 oz/540 mL) chickpeas, drained and rinsed	1
¼ cup	chopped fresh cilantro or parsley	50 mL

1. In casserole dish, combine oil, potatoes, onion, garlic, chili powder, cumin, salt and hot pepper flakes, if using. Microwave, covered, on High for 5 to 8 minutes, stirring once, until potatoes are almost tender.

2. Add tomatoes with juice and chickpeas. Microwave, covered, on High for 8 to 12 minutes, stirring once, until potatoes are tender.

3. Stir in cilantro. Let stand, covered, for 3 minutes before serving.

Easy Baked Beans

Here's a spruced-up bean dish flavored with bacon that uses a handy can of baked beans. No one will know that it wasn't made from scratch.

8-cup (2 L) casserole dish with lid

4	slices bacon, chopped	4
1	onion, finely chopped	1
1	can (28 oz/796 mL) beans in tomato sauce	1
¼ cup	packed brown sugar	50 mL
¼ cup	ketchup	50 mL
1 tbsp	Worcestershire sauce	15 mL
1 tsp	Dijon mustard	5 mL

1. In a casserole dish, microwave bacon, uncovered, on High for 2 to 3 minutes or until partially cooked. Drain off excess fat in dish. Add onions and microwave, uncovered, on High for 2 to 3 minutes, stirring once, until bacon is crisp and onions are tender.

2. Add beans, brown sugar, ketchup, Worcestershire sauce and mustard. Microwave, covered, on High for 5 to 8 minutes, stirring once, or until heated through. Let stand, covered, for 2 minutes before serving.

Chili Black Bean Wraps

These vegetarian wraps are ideal to pack for lunch because they can be eaten either warm or cold, depending on whether there's a microwave on hand.

Tip

Bean filling can be covered and refrigerated for up to 3 days or frozen for up to 2 months.

4-cup (1 L) casserole dish with lid

1 tbsp	vegetable or olive oil	15 mL
1	small onion, chopped	1
1	large clove garlic, minced	1
1	large green bell pepper, chopped	1
1½ tsp	chili powder	7 mL
½ tsp	ground cumin	2 mL
½ tsp	dried oregano leaves	2 mL
1	can (19 oz/540 mL) black beans or kidney beans, drained and rinsed	1
½ cup	mild or medium salsa	125 mL
¼ cup	chopped fresh cilantro	50 mL
6	large (9-inch/23 cm) flour tortillas	6
1½ cups	shredded mozzarella or Cheddar cheese, divided	375 mL
2	tomatoes, thinly sliced, divided	2
3 cups	shredded romaine lettuce, divided	750 mL

1. In casserole dish, combine oil, onion, garlic, green pepper, chili powder, cumin and oregano. Microwave, covered, on High for 2 to 3 minutes or until softened.

2. In a bowl, coarsely mash half of the beans with a fork. Stir in onion mixture, remaining beans, salsa and cilantro. Spread scant ½ cup (125 mL) bean mixture along bottom half of each flour tortilla. Sprinkle each evenly with cheese, tomato slices and lettuce. Fold 1 inch (2.5 cm) of left and right sides over filling and roll up.

3. Wraps can be eaten cold or warm. Place 3 wraps at a time, seam side down, on paper towel–lined plate. Microwave, uncovered, on Medium-High (70%) for 1½ to 2 minutes or until warm to the touch. Repeat with remaining wraps.

> **Micro-Tip**
>
> To make ahead, complete recipe to Step 2. Wrap sandwiches individually in plastic wrap and store in the refrigerator for up to 1 day. To warm individual wraps, remove plastic and wrap in a paper towel. Microwave on Medium-High (70%) for 45 to 60 seconds.

Curried Lentil Stew with Vegetables

Serves 4

Heady with the fragrance of curry, this one-pot stew made with convenient canned lentils is a substantial meal in a bowl.

Variation

This is a meatless stew but you can add about 1½ cups (375 mL) diced cooked roast lamb, pork or ham along with lentils.

8-cup (2 L) casserole dish with lid

1 tbsp	vegetable oil	15 mL
1	onion, chopped	1
2	cloves garlic, minced	2
1 tbsp	minced fresh gingerroot	15 mL
1 tbsp	mild curry paste or powder, or to taste	15 mL
Pinch	cayenne pepper	Pinch
2 cups	diced peeled potatoes (about 2)	500 mL
1½ cups	thinly sliced carrots (about 3)	375 mL
1½ cups	vegetable or chicken stock	375 mL
¼ cup	tomato paste	50 mL
1	can (19 oz/540 mL) lentils, drained and rinsed	1
	Salt and freshly ground black pepper	
¼ cup	chopped fresh cilantro or parsley	50 mL
	Plain yogurt (optional)	

1. In casserole dish, combine oil, onion, garlic, ginger, curry paste and cayenne pepper. Microwave, covered, on High for 2 to 3 minutes, until onion is softened.

2. Add potatoes, carrots, stock and tomato paste. Microwave, covered, on High for 10 to 14 minutes, stirring once, until vegetables are tender.

3. Add lentils. Microwave, covered, on High for 3 to 5 minutes or until piping hot. Season with salt, if required, and pepper to taste.

4. Sprinkle with cilantro and serve in heated bowls. Top each with a spoonful of yogurt, if desired.

Vegetable Barley Casserole

■ Traditionally used in soups, barley also makes a hearty grain dish to serve with roasted meats or to stand alone as a vegetarian dish.

Tip

Parsley adds color and flavor to many dishes, but it can be tedious to chop for each recipe. Here's a way to save time: Wash a fresh bunch of parsley well, remove the tough stems and spin the top sprigs in a salad spinner to remove as much moisture as possible. Chop the parsley in batches in a food processor or by hand and place in a covered container in the freezer. Whenever a recipe calls for parsley, measure out the amount needed and add to casseroles, stews and soups.

8-cup (2 L) casserole dish with lid

1	onion, chopped	1
1 cup	sliced mushrooms	250 mL
1	large carrot, peeled and diced	1
1	stalk celery, chopped	1
1/4 tsp	dried thyme leaves	1 mL
1 tbsp	olive or vegetable oil	15 mL
1 cup	pearl barley, rinsed	250 mL
2 cups	chicken or vegetable stock	500 mL
1/4 cup	chopped fresh parsley (see Tip, left)	50 mL
	Salt and freshly ground black pepper	

1. In casserole dish, combine onion, mushrooms, carrot, celery and thyme. Drizzle with oil. Microwave, covered, on High for 4 to 6 minutes, stirring once, until vegetables are softened.

2. Add barley and stock. Microwave, covered, on High for 5 to 7 minutes or until boiling. Reduce to Medium (50%) and microwave for 16 to 20 minutes or until barley is tender and liquid is absorbed. Stir in parsley. Season with salt and pepper to taste. Let stand, covered, for 5 minutes before serving.

Italian Couscous with Zucchini and Red Pepper

Serves 4 to 6

Couscous, like pasta, is made from semolina, with the added benefit that it only needs to be reconstituted in boiling stock or liquid before serving. It's available in most supermarkets and in bulk food shops.

Tip

Dice the zucchini and red pepper into ¼-inch (0.5 cm) pieces.

8-cup (2 L) casserole dish with lid

1 tbsp	olive oil	15 mL
1	small onion, chopped	1
1½ cups	diced zucchini (about 1)	375 mL
1	red bell pepper, diced	1
1½ cups	vegetable or chicken stock	375 mL
1 tsp	dried basil leaves	5 mL
1½ cups	regular or whole wheat couscous	375 mL
⅓ cup	freshly grated Parmesan cheese	75 mL
	Salt and freshly ground black pepper	

1. In casserole dish, combine oil, onion, zucchini and red pepper. Microwave, covered, on High for 3 to 5 minutes or until vegetables are softened.

2. Stir in stock and basil. Microwave, covered, on High for 4 to 6 minutes or until stock comes to a full boil.

3. Stir in couscous. Let stand, covered, for 5 minutes. Fluff with fork. Add Parmesan. Season with salt and pepper to taste.

Bulgur Pilaf with Apple and Cilantro

Bulgur is precooked cracked wheat that has been dried. It has become a staple in most supermarkets thanks to the popularity of Middle Eastern cuisine. The fine-textured variety is preferred when making the Lebanese salad tabbouleh. I prefer the coarser-textured bulgur when making this pleasing side dish to serve with pork or chicken or as a main-course vegetarian dish.

8-cup (2 L) casserole dish with lid

2 tsp	butter	10 mL
2	green onions, sliced	2
1	apple, peeled and finely diced	1
1 tsp	ground cumin or coriander	5 mL
1 cup	coarse-grain bulgur	250 mL
1½ cups	chicken stock	375 mL
¼ cup	dried cranberries	50 mL
2 tbsp	chopped fresh cilantro or parsley	25 mL
	Salt and freshly ground black pepper	

1. In casserole dish, combine butter, green onions, apple and cumin. Microwave, covered, on High for 3 to 5 minutes, stirring once, until apple is tender.

2. Stir in bulgur, stock and cranberries. Microwave, covered, on High for 4 to 6 minutes or until stock comes to a boil. Reduce to Medium (50%) and microwave for 6 to 9 minutes or until most of the liquid is absorbed.

3. Let stand, covered, for 5 minutes before serving. Stir in cilantro. Season with salt and pepper to taste.

Micro-Tip

Let cool, then cover and refrigerate for up to 2 days. To reheat, add 1 to 2 tbsp (15 to 25 mL) water and microwave, covered, on High for 2 to 3 minutes or until piping hot.

Creamy Polenta

Polenta is Italian comfort food — a creamy cornmeal porridge that is wonderful served with any kind of a meat or vegetable pasta sauce or swirled with basil pesto sauce and extra Parmesan. Another serving suggestion is to cut cold polenta into squares and grill it alongside other vegetables such as peppers and zucchini, and Italian sausages.

Tips

To prepare polenta for grilling, prepare recipe as directed but reduce water to 1 cup (250 mL) to make a thicker polenta. Add Parmesan cheese and omit the butter. Spread in oiled 10-cup (2.5 L) shallow baking dish and let stand for 30 minutes or until firm. Cut into squares or rectangles. Brush lightly with olive oil and place on a hot greased grill or stovetop grill, or in a nonstick skillet until lightly colored.

If using only water when making polenta, add 1 tsp (5 mL) salt.

8-cup (2 L) casserole dish with lid

1½ cups	chicken stock or water	375 mL
1½ cups	water	375 mL
¾ cup	yellow cornmeal	175 mL
¼ cup	freshly grated Parmesan cheese	50 mL
2 tbsp	butter	25 mL
	Salt (optional)	

1. Place stock and water in casserole dish. Stir in cornmeal. Microwave, covered, on High for 10 to 14 minutes, stirring well with a wooden spoon every 3 minutes, until thickened and creamy.

2. Stir in Parmesan and butter. Season with salt, if necessary.

Vegetables and Salads

Baked Potatoes with Broccoli Cheese Sauce

Serves 4

A large baked potato either stuffed or with a sauce makes a tasty and economical meal. Complete the menu with a salad tossed with a variety of crisp greens followed by a fruit dessert such as Maple Baked Apples (see recipe, page 171).

8-cup (2 L) glass measure
8-cup (2 L) casserole dish with lid

4	large baking potatoes (each 10 oz/300 g)	4
2 tbsp	butter	25 mL
2 tbsp	all-purpose flour	25 mL
1¼ cups	milk	300 mL
1 tsp	Dijon mustard	5 mL
1 cup	shredded Gruyère or Cheddar cheese	250 mL
¼ tsp	salt	1 mL
	Freshly ground black pepper	
4 cups	finely chopped broccoli florets	1 L

1. Microwave potatoes as directed in Micro-Tips (see page 123).

2. In glass measure, melt butter, uncovered, on High for 30 to 45 seconds or until bubbling. Blend in flour. Stir in milk and mustard until smooth. Microwave, uncovered, on High for 3 to 4 minutes, stirring once, until sauce comes to a full rolling boil. Stir in cheese until melted. Season with salt, and pepper to taste. Set aside.

3. Place broccoli in casserole dish with ¼ cup (50 mL) water. Microwave, covered, on High for 3 to 4 minutes or until bright green and tender-crisp. Drain well. Stir into cheese sauce. Reheat sauce, if necessary, uncovered, on High for 1 minute.

4. Slice potatoes in half lengthwise and place on serving plates. Spoon sauce over top and serve.

Tuna-Stuffed Potatoes

Serves 2

Can't bear to see another bagged tuna sandwich for lunch? Try these tuna-stuffed potatoes instead. They're ideal to make ahead and pop into the microwave for a quick reheat.

Bacon rack (optional)

2	baking potatoes (each 8 to 10 oz/250 to 300 g)	2
1	can (6½ oz/170 g) solid white or light tuna, drained and flaked	1
1	stalk celery, chopped	1
1	green onion, sliced	1
⅓ cup	sour cream or plain yogurt	75 mL
½ cup	shredded Cheddar cheese, divided	125 mL
	Salt and freshly ground black pepper	

1. Microwave potatoes as directed in Micro-Tips (see below).

2. Cut each potato in half lengthwise and scoop out potato leaving a ¼-inch (0.5 cm) shell. Place in a bowl and mash. Add tuna, celery, onion, sour cream and half of the cheese. Season with salt and pepper to taste. Spoon mixture back into shells and sprinkle tops with remaining cheese.

3. Arrange on rack or plate and microwave, uncovered, on Medium (50%) for 2½ to 4 minutes or until heated through and cheese melts.

Micro-Tips

To microwave baking potatoes

1. Scrub potatoes well. Because the potato's skin is a natural wrapping that prevents moisture loss, it's necessary to pierce in several places with a fork to allow steam to escape or else skins will burst during cooking. Arrange potatoes in a circle, spacing 1 inch (2.5 cm) apart on a bacon rack or on a paper towel on turntable or floor of microwave oven.

2. Microwave, uncovered, on High until potatoes give slightly when squeezed, turning halfway through and rearranging once during cooking. After cooking, if you prefer a moist potato, wrap each cooked potato individually in foil. For a drier potato, wrap in a dry kitchen towel. Let stand for 5 minutes.

Here are cooking times for large baking potatoes (average size 10 oz/300 g) cooked on High:

1 potato	4 to 6 minutes
2 potatoes	6 to 9 minutes
4 potatoes	10 to 14 minutes

Baked Pizza Potatoes

Rather than being tempted to order in on those harried nights when you need to have dinner in a hurry, have baking potatoes on hand to serve with this easy pizza-style topping for supper that's ready in 30 minutes.

Tip

Serve this versatile pizza sauce over tube-shaped pasta such as rigatoni and top with freshly grated Parmesan cheese for a quick supper idea. Or spread sauce over 4 split crusty Kaiser rolls. Place 2 rolls at a time on paper towel-lined plate and microwave on Medium (50%), uncovered, for 1 to 1$\frac{1}{2}$ minutes or until melted. Or place rolls on a baking sheet and place under a preheated broiler until cheese melts.

4-cup (1 L) casserole dish with lid

4	large baking potatoes (each 10 oz/300 g)	4
1 tbsp	olive oil	15 mL
1	small onion, chopped	1
1	clove garlic, minced	1
1	green bell pepper, finely chopped	1
1 cup	sliced mushrooms	250 mL
1 tsp	dried oregano leaves	5 mL
1	can (14 oz/398 mL) pizza sauce	1
$\frac{1}{2}$ cup	sliced pepperoni, cut into thin strips (optional)	125 mL
1 cup	shredded mozzarella cheese	250 mL

1. Microwave potatoes as directed in Micro-Tips (see page 123). Let stand, covered, while preparing sauce.

2. In casserole dish, combine oil, onion, garlic, green pepper, mushrooms and oregano. Microwave, covered, on High for 4 to 6 minutes, stirring once, until vegetables are tender. Stir in pizza sauce and pepperoni strips, if using. Microwave, covered, on High for 3 to 5 minutes or until sauce is piping hot.

3. Cut potatoes in half lengthwise and arrange on individual serving plates. Spoon hot pizza sauce over top and sprinkle with cheese. Microwave each plate, uncovered, on High for 45 to 60 seconds or until cheese melts.

Scalloped Potatoes

For old-fashioned comfort cooking, count on these potatoes — always a mealtime favorite.

Tip

If desired, place casserole under preheated broiler, 4 inches (10 cm) from source of heat, until cheese melts and is bubbling.

Variation

Scalloped Potatoes with Ham and Cheese For a simple meal-in-one dish, add 1 cup (250 mL) diced baked ham to potatoes.

8-cup (2 L) glass measure
8-inch (2 L) square baking dish, buttered

1½ cups	milk	375 mL
2 tbsp	butter	25 mL
2 tbsp	all-purpose flour	25 mL
1 tsp	Dijon mustard	5 mL
½ tsp	salt	2 mL
	Freshly ground black pepper	
4	potatoes, thinly sliced (1½ lbs/750 g)	4
1	small onion, halved lengthwise and thinly sliced	1
½ cup	shredded Swiss or Cheddar cheese	125 mL

1. In glass measure, heat milk, uncovered, on High for 2½ to 4 minutes or until piping hot but not boiling.

2. In small bowl, melt butter, uncovered, on High for 30 to 45 seconds or until bubbling. Blend in flour and mustard. Whisk into hot milk mixture. Microwave, uncovered, on High for 2½ to 4 minutes, stirring once, until sauce comes to a full boil and thickens. Season with salt, and pepper to taste.

3. Stir in sliced potatoes and onion and coat in sauce. Spread in prepared baking dish. Cover with plastic wrap and turn back one corner to vent. Microwave on High for 10 to 15 minutes or until potatoes are just tender when pierced with tip of sharp knife.

4. Sprinkle with cheese. Microwave, uncovered, for 1 to 2 minutes, until cheese melts. Let stand for 5 minutes before serving.

Buttermilk Mashed Potatoes

You'll appreciate this no-fuss way of cooking potatoes and counting on your microwave to handle some of the cooking chores when preparing dinner.

8-cup (2 L) casserole dish with lid

2 tbsp	butter	25 mL
1	small onion, chopped	1
2	cloves garlic, minced	2
2 lbs	potatoes, peeled and quartered (about 6)	1 kg
1/4 cup	chicken stock	50 mL
1/2 cup	buttermilk or sour cream (approx.)	125 mL
	Salt and freshly ground black pepper	
	Freshly grated nutmeg	

1. In casserole dish, combine butter, onion and garlic. Microwave, covered, on High for 2 to 3 minutes or until onion is softened.

2. Add potatoes and stock. Microwave, covered, on High for 12 to 16 minutes, stirring once, until potatoes are very tender. Do not drain. Transfer to a bowl.

3. Mash potatoes with potato masher or electric hand mixer. Add enough buttermilk to make a smooth purée. Season with salt, pepper and nutmeg to taste. Spoon potatoes back into casserole dish. Cover and reheat on High for 2 to 4 minutes or until piping hot.

Micro-Tip

To cut down on last-minute dishes, make mashed potatoes a day ahead and reheat. Season with salt and pepper, and be sure to add extra milk or buttermilk to keep them creamy as potatoes become dry when cool. Cream cheese, sour cream or grated Cheddar cheese can also be added to help keep mashed potatoes moist. Cover and refrigerate for up to 1 day.

To reheat, microwave, covered, on Medium-High (70%) for 5 to 8 minutes or until heated through. Time will depend on amount of potatoes and size of casserole dish. Check center of dish to make sure mashed potatoes are piping hot.

Garlic and Cheese Mashed Sweet Potatoes

Serves 4

■ Most recipes team sweet potatoes with sugar and other fruit mixtures. As a substitute for mashed potatoes, try these delicious mashed sweet potatoes with garlic and cheese. I like to serve them with baked ham basted with a honey mustard glaze or with roast pork.

8-cup (2 L) casserole dish with lid

3	medium or 2 large sweet potatoes (about 2 lbs/1 kg)	3
1/3 cup	chicken stock (approx.)	75 mL
1 tbsp	butter	15 mL
1	clove garlic, minced	1
1/2 cup	shredded Cheddar, Swiss or Havarti cheese	125 mL
	Salt and freshly ground black pepper	

1. Peel potatoes and cut into 1-inch (2.5 cm) cubes. Place in casserole dish with stock. Microwave, covered, on High for 7 to 11 minutes, stirring once, until tender. Do not drain. Using a potato masher or electric hand mixer, mash, adding more stock if necessary to make a smooth purée.

2. In small glass dish, microwave butter and garlic, uncovered, on High for 20 to 30 seconds or until fragrant. Drizzle over potato mixture and stir in cheese. Season with salt and pepper to taste. Microwave, covered, on High for 2 to 3 minutes or until piping hot.

Micro-Tips

■ Recipe can be made up to 2 days ahead, covered and refrigerated. To reheat, microwave, covered, on Medium-High (70%) for 5 to 8 minutes or until piping hot.

■ How to micro-bake sweet potatoes
Scrub and pierce the skins of sweet potatoes in several places with fork to prevent the buildup of steam that may cause them to pop or explode in your microwave.

Place on a rack or plate lined with double thickness of paper towels. Arrange in a circle with some space between each potato. Microwave, uncovered, on High, turning once halfway through cooking, for the following times or until tender when pierced with fork. Times vary with size and shape of potatoes. Once cooked, let stand, covered with a dry towel, for 5 minutes.

1 medium sweet potato (12 oz/375 g)	4 to 6 minutes
2 potatoes (1 1/2 lbs/750 g)	7 to 9 minutes
3 potatoes (2 1/4 lbs/1.125 kg)	10 to 13 minutes

Broccoli with Orange Sauce

Serves 4

I wouldn't think of any other way of cooking broccoli than in the microwave as it keeps its vibrant color and crispness.

8-cup (2 L) casserole dish with lid

5 to 6 cups	broccoli florets and stems, cut into 2-inch (5 cm) pieces	1.25 to 1.5 L
1 tbsp	butter	15 mL
1 tsp	grated orange zest	5 mL
2 tbsp	freshly squeezed orange juice	25 mL
2 tsp	red wine vinegar	10 mL
1 tsp	Dijon mustard	5 mL
1/2 tsp	granulated sugar	2 mL
1/2 tsp	cornstarch	2 mL
	Salt and freshly ground black pepper	

1. Place broccoli in casserole dish and add 1/3 cup (75 mL) water. Microwave, covered, on High for 4 to 6 minutes or until bright green and just tender-crisp. Let stand, covered, while making sauce.

2. In a small glass measure, combine butter, orange zest and juice, vinegar, mustard and sugar. Stir in cornstarch until smooth. Microwave, uncovered, on High for 40 to 60 seconds, stirring once, until sauce boils and thickens.

3. Drain broccoli well. Pour sauce over top and toss to coat. Season with salt and pepper to taste.

Micro-Tip

Broccoli is an excellent vegetable to cook in the microwave oven. Cut into equal-size florets, trim the stalks and cut into smaller pieces. Place tender florets toward center of your dish with the thicker and denser stalks positioned to the outside. Add 1 tbsp (15 mL) water for each cup (250 mL) of broccoli. Cover dish with lid, dinner plate or plastic wrap with one corner turned back to vent. Use your microwave oven's sensor cook feature or estimate 4 to 6 minutes per lb (9 to 13 minutes per kg) of trimmed broccoli, cooked on High.

Spicy Spaghettini with Peppers and Olives (page 99)

Overleaf: Buttermilk Mashed Potatoes (page 126) and Company Vegetables with Toasted Almonds (page 132)

Brussels Sprouts with Parmesan Cheese Sauce

Serves 6		

Brussels sprouts cook up perfectly in the microwave. This do-ahead recipe helps cut down on last-minute dinner preparation and is ideal to serve for holiday meals such as Thanksgiving. Serve this lemon-accented cream sauce with other cooked vegetables, such as cauliflower or broccoli.

Variation

You can substitute cauliflower for the Brussels sprouts. Separate 1 cauliflower into florets (about 6 cups/1.5 L). Place in casserole dish with 1/3 cup (75 mL) water. Microwave, covered, on High for 6 to 9 minutes, stirring once, until just tender. Prepare sauce as directed. Drain cauliflower and toss with sauce.

8-cup (2 L) casserole dish with lid
8-cup (2 L) glass measure

1 1/2 lbs	Brussels sprouts, ends trimmed and cut in half lengthwise	750 g
2 tbsp	butter	25 mL
2 tbsp	all-purpose flour	25 mL
1 1/3 cups	milk	325 mL
1/4 cup	freshly grated Parmesan cheese	50 mL
1 tsp	grated lemon zest	5 mL
	Salt	
	Freshly grated nutmeg	

1. Place Brussels sprouts in casserole dish and add 1/3 cup (75 mL) water. Microwave, covered, on High for 5 to 8 minutes, stirring once, until just tender and bright green. Let stand, covered, while making sauce.

2. In glass measure, melt butter, uncovered, on High for 30 to 45 seconds or until bubbling. Blend in flour. Whisk in milk. Microwave, uncovered, on High for 3 to 4 minutes, whisking once, until sauce comes to a full rolling boil and thickens.

3. Add Parmesan cheese and lemon zest. Season with salt and nutmeg to taste. Drain Brussels sprouts well and pour sauce over top.

Micro-Tips

To make ahead, prepare recipe as directed earlier in the day, cover and refrigerate. To reheat, microwave, covered, on High for 4 to 7 minutes, stirring once, until piping hot.

Milk-based sauces tend to boil over, so prepare them in a large glass measure.

To cook whole Brussels sprouts in the microwave, trim ends and cut a small X on the bottom of each sprout. Add 1/3 cup (75 mL) water. Microwave, covered, on High for 6 to 9 minutes, stirring once, until just tender and bright green.

Asparagus Salad with Gorgonzola (page 147)

Stewed Zucchini and Red Pepper

For a quick supper, toss this vegetable sauce with 8 oz (250 g) cooked pasta and sprinkle with Parmesan cheese.

Tip

Add 2 tbsp (25 mL) chopped fresh basil instead of dried basil leaves and stir in when zucchini is tender.

8-cup (2 L) casserole dish with lid

2 tbsp	olive oil	25 mL
1	onion, halved lengthwise and thinly sliced	1
1	large clove garlic, minced	1
3/4 tsp	dried basil leaves	4 mL
1/4 tsp	hot pepper flakes (optional)	1 mL
3	small zucchini, halved lengthwise and thinly sliced	3
2	tomatoes, seeded and chopped	2
1	small red bell pepper, diced	1
	Salt and freshly ground black pepper	

1. In casserole dish, combine oil, onion, garlic, basil and hot pepper flakes, if using. Microwave, covered, on High for 2 to 3 minutes or until onion is softened.

2. Add zucchini, tomatoes and red pepper. Microwave, covered, on High for 5 to 8 minutes, stirring once, until zucchini is barely tender. Season with salt and pepper to taste. Let stand, covered, for 2 minutes.

Rutabaga with Parmesan Crumb Topping

This is a great make-ahead dish to serve with Sunday pork roast or for holiday turkey.

8-cup (2 L) casserole dish with lid
4-cup (1 L) casserole dish with lid

1	medium rutabaga (about 6 to 8 cups/1.5 to 2 L), peeled and cut into ¾-inch (2 cm) cubes	1
2 tbsp	brown sugar or to taste	25 mL
	Salt and freshly ground black pepper	
1 tbsp	butter	15 mL
⅓ cup	freshly grated Parmesan cheese	75 mL
3 tbsp	fine dry bread crumbs (see Micro-Tip, below)	45 mL
1 tbsp	chopped fresh parsley	15 mL

1. In large casserole dish, combine rutabaga with ¾ cup (175 mL) water. Microwave, covered, on High for 15 to 20 minutes, stirring twice, until tender. Let stand, covered, for 10 minutes.

2. Drain well and mash using a potato masher or place in a food processor until quite smooth (not a purée). Add brown sugar, salt and pepper to taste. Place in 4-cup (1 L) casserole dish. Cover and refrigerate for up to 2 days ahead.

3. Microwave, covered, on Medium-High (70%) for 6 to 9 minutes, stirring once, until piping hot.

4. In a microwave-safe bowl, microwave butter, uncovered, on High for 15 to 20 seconds until melted. Stir in Parmesan, bread crumbs and parsley. Smooth top of rutabaga and sprinkle with crumb topping. Place under preheated broiler until crumbs are lightly browned.

Micro-Tip

How to make dry bread crumbs in your microwave: Place 4 slices stale white or whole wheat bread on double paper towel–lined dinner plate. Microwave, uncovered, on High for 2½ to 4 minutes, turning slices once, until crisp. Watch carefully to prevent bread from scorching. Let cool completely. Break into pieces and place in food processor to make fine crumbs. Or, place in heavy plastic bag and use a rolling pin to make fine crumbs.

Company Vegetables with Toasted Almonds

Put your microwave oven to good use when preparing vegetables to serve a crowd. Arrange vegetables in dish, ready to pop in the microwave shortly before serving. Serve almond butter with other steamed vegetables, such as Brussels sprouts.

Variation

Substitute partially cooked carrots for the pepper cubes, if desired. To prepare, place 3 cups (750 mL) thinly sliced carrots and $1/4$ cup (50 mL) water in a casserole dish. Microwave, covered, on High for 2 to 4 minutes or until crisp. Drain and continue with recipe as directed.

10-cup (2.5 L) shallow baking dish or large (12-inch/30 cm) microwave-safe platter (see Micro-Tip, right)

4 cups	cauliflower florets ($1/2$ head)	1 L
4 cups	broccoli florets	1 L
1	red bell pepper, cut into cubes	1
1	yellow or orange bell pepper, cut into cubes	1

TOPPING

3 tbsp	butter, divided	45 mL
$1/3$ cup	sliced almonds	75 mL
1	clove garlic, minced	1
1 tbsp	freshly squeezed lemon juice	15 mL
2 tbsp	chopped fresh parsley	25 mL
	Salt and freshly ground black pepper	

1. In baking dish or platter, alternately arrange cauliflower and broccoli, with broccoli stalks toward the outside, around outer edge of dish. Mound pepper cubes in center. Add $1/3$ cup (75 mL) water. Cover with lid or plastic wrap and turn back one corner to vent. Microwave on High for 6 to 9 minutes or until vegetables are tender-crisp. Let stand, covered, while preparing topping.

2. *Topping:* In a small microwave-safe glass bowl, combine 2 tbsp (25 mL) of the butter and almonds. Microwave, uncovered, on High for $1 1/2$ to 3 minutes or until almonds are lightly toasted, stirring twice. (Can be done up to 4 hours ahead, if desired.)

3. Just before serving, add remaining butter and garlic to toasted almonds. Microwave, uncovered, on High for 45 to 60 seconds or until fragrant. Stir in lemon juice. Carefully drain water from vegetables (a plate set on top will hold vegetables in place).

4. Pour almond butter over top. Sprinkle with parsley. Season with salt and pepper to taste. Serve immediately.

Micro-Tip

■ Test first to see if dish called for fits comfortably in your microwave oven. If not, divide vegetable mixture among two 9-inch (23 cm) microwave-safe pie plates. Cover with inverted plate or plastic wrap with one corner turned back to vent. Microwave each plate on High for 4 to 6 minutes.

Creamed Corn with Chives

Serves 4

Whether served simply with a slather of butter and dash of salt or dressed up as in this recipe with a touch of cream and fresh herbs, just-picked corn on the cob is one of the summer's best treats. To cut kernels from cobs, stand ears on end and cut straight down using a sharp paring knife.

8-cup (2 L) casserole dish with lid

3 cups	uncooked corn kernels (5 or 6 cobs) or frozen corn	750 mL
1/3 cup	whipping (35%) cream	75 mL
1 1/2 tsp	cornstarch	7 mL
1/4 cup	chicken stock (approx.)	50 mL
	Salt	
	Freshly grated nutmeg	
2 tbsp	chopped fresh chives, basil or parsley	25 mL

1. In casserole dish, combine corn and cream. Microwave, covered, on High for 3 to 5 minutes (5 to 7 minutes, if frozen), stirring once, until corn is almost tender.

2. In a small bowl, blend cornstarch with stock. Stir into corn. Microwave, covered, for 2 to 3 minutes, stirring once, until corn is tender and sauce is thickened. Season with salt and nutmeg to taste. Thin with additional stock, if needed. Sprinkle with chives. Let stand, covered, for 2 minutes before serving.

Micro-Tips

To cook corn right in the husk: Leave husks intact and rinse corn under cold water for added moisture. Arrange 2 inches (5 cm) apart directly on floor of microwave oven. Microwave on High for the following times:
(Note: Cooking times may vary according to size and maturity of corn, for large cobs, increase time slightly):

1 cob	2 1/2 to 3 minutes
2 cobs	4 to 5 minutes
3 cobs	6 to 8 minutes
4 cobs	8 to 10 minutes

Turn cobs over and rearrange halfway through cooking. Let stand for 3 minutes, then pull away silk and husk. Butter and salt, if desired, and serve.

For even cooking, do not microwave more than 4 ears of corn at a time.

To cook corn on the cob with silk and husk removed: Place corn in a single layer in a shallow casserole dish, add 1/4 cup (50 mL) water and cover with lid or plastic wrap and turn back one corner to vent. Microwave according to times indicated above, turning over and rearranging corn halfway through cooking.

Orange Ginger Carrots

Serves 4

Like fresh garlic, fresh gingerroot has now become a kitchen staple that enhances a variety of dishes. Here, it teams with the vibrant spark of orange to perk up baby carrots.

Tips

Recipe can be made earlier in day. Cover and refrigerate. Reheat on High for 2 to 4 minutes or until piping hot.

Serve this tasty Orange Ginger Sauce with other cooked vegetables such as cooked sliced beets, broccoli and snow peas.

8-cup (2 L) casserole dish with lid

1 lb	whole baby carrots	500 g

ORANGE GINGER SAUCE

1 tbsp	butter	15 mL
2 tsp	minced fresh gingerroot	10 mL
1 tsp	grated orange zest	5 mL
1/4 cup	freshly squeezed orange juice	50 mL
1/2 tsp	cornstarch	2 mL
1/2 tsp	granulated sugar	2 mL
	Salt and freshly ground black pepper	
1 tbsp	chopped fresh parsley or chives	15 mL

1. In casserole dish, combine carrots and 1/4 cup (50 mL) water. Microwave, covered, on High for 5 to 8 minutes, stirring once, until carrots are just tender. Let stand, covered, while making sauce.

2. *Orange Ginger Sauce:* In a small bowl or glass measure, combine butter and ginger. Microwave, uncovered, on High for 40 to 60 seconds, until ginger is softened. Stir in orange zest and juice, cornstarch and sugar until smooth. Microwave, uncovered, on High for 1 to 1 1/2 minutes, stirring once, until sauce boils and thickens. Season with salt and pepper to taste.

3. Drain carrots well and pour sauce over top. Sprinkle with parsley and serve.

Asian Vegetable Medley

Serves 4

When the price of imported fresh produce skyrockets, frozen vegetables are a convenient and economical alternative for the busy cook. There are several good combinations of frozen stir-fry vegetables in supermarkets. I prefer the ones with snow peas, broccoli and red pepper as part of the mix to use in this recipe.

Tip

Bottled minced ginger is a great timesaver for cooks who prefer the taste of fresh ginger to the ground version.

8-cup (2 L) casserole dish with lid

¼ cup	water or chicken stock	50 mL
2 tbsp	soy sauce	25 mL
1	small clove garlic, minced	1
1 tsp	minced fresh gingerroot (see Tip, left)	5 mL
½ tsp	granulated sugar	2 mL
1½ tsp	cornstarch	7 mL
1	package (1 lb/500 g) frozen Asian mixed vegetables (4 cups/1 L)	1

1. In casserole dish, combine water, soy sauce, garlic, ginger and sugar. Blend in cornstarch until smooth. Microwave, uncovered, on High for 1½ to 2 minutes, stirring once, until sauce is very thick.

2. Stir in frozen vegetables, coating well with sauce. Microwave, covered, on High for 6 to 9 minutes, stirring once, until vegetables are just tender. Let stand, covered, for 2 minutes before serving.

Micro-Tip

To cook frozen vegetables: Remove packaging and place vegetables in covered casserole dish. Refer to package directions regarding adding water. For individual quick-cooking vegetables, such as corn and peas, add 1 tbsp (15 mL) water or stock per cup (250 mL) of vegetables. The added moisture helps create steam during cooking. Microwave on High according to package directions (usually 4 to 7 minutes for 10 oz/300 g package). Stir halfway through cooking so vegetables cook evenly.

Red Cabbage with Apples

Red cabbage is an economical wintertime vegetable that makes a great-tasting side dish you can make ahead of time. It freezes well, too.

12-cup (3 L) casserole dish with lid

1	onion, chopped	1
1/3 cup	packed brown sugar	75 mL
1/4 cup	red wine vinegar	50 mL
1/4 cup	chicken stock or water	50 mL
2 tsp	cornstarch	10 mL
1	cinnamon stick, broken into 2 pieces	1
6 cups	shredded red cabbage (about 1/2 head)	1.5 L
2	apples, peeled, cored and chopped	2
1/2 tsp	salt	2 mL
	Freshly ground black pepper	

1. In casserole dish, combine onion, brown sugar, vinegar, stock and cornstarch until smooth. Add cinnamon stick. Microwave, covered, on High for 2 to 3 minutes or until sauce is thickened.

2. Stir in cabbage and apples. Season with salt, and pepper to taste. Microwave, covered, on High for 13 to 18 minutes, stirring once, until cabbage is tender.

3. Let stand, covered, for 5 minutes. Remove cinnamon stick before serving.

Fennel with Tomatoes and Black Olives

Sometimes referred to as anise in supermarkets, fennel, with its frond-like top, is a popular vegetable used in Italian cooking. Similar to celery in texture, it has a mild licorice flavor that disappears when cooked.

Tip

To prepare fennel for cooking or to use raw in salads, trim bottom and cut off the herb-like top. Halve lengthwise and cut into thin wedges.

Variation

For an easy supper suggestion, toss cooked fennel with pasta, such as penne, and freshly grated Parmesan or Romano cheese.

8-cup (2 L) casserole dish with lid

1 tbsp	olive oil	15 mL
1	small onion, chopped	1
2	cloves garlic, minced	2
5 cups	fennel strips (2 bulbs)	1.25 L
2	ripe tomatoes, peeled, seeded and diced (see Micro-Tip, below)	2
1/3 cup	dry-cured black olives (optional)	75 mL
	Salt and freshly ground black pepper	

1. In casserole dish, combine oil, onion and garlic. Microwave, covered, on High for 2 to 3 minutes or until softened. Add fennel strips, tomatoes and olives, if using.

2. Microwave, covered, on High for 7 to 11 minutes, stirring once, until fennel is tender-crisp. Season with salt and pepper to taste. Let stand, covered, for 2 minutes before serving.

Micro-Tip

To peel tomatoes: Place 1 cup (250 mL) hot tap water in a 2-cup (500 mL) glass measure. Microwave on High for $1\frac{1}{2}$ to $2\frac{1}{2}$ minutes or until boiling. Remove core from tomato and discard. Carefully place one tomato in boiling water. Microwave on High for 20 to 40 seconds until skin loosens. Repeat for each tomato.

Summer Vegetables with Basil

The microwave preserves the fresh summer flavors in this colorful vegetable dish accented with fresh herbs.

8-cup (2 L) casserole dish with lid

2 cups	uncooked corn kernels (3 to 4 cobs)	500 mL
1	red bell pepper, finely diced	1
1	zucchini, finely diced	1
1 tbsp	butter	15 mL
	Salt and freshly ground black pepper	
2 tbsp	chopped fresh herbs such basil, parsley or chives	25 mL

1. In casserole dish, combine corn, red pepper and zucchini. Dot with butter. Microwave, covered, on High for 5 to 7 minutes or until vegetables are just tender.
2. Season with salt and pepper to taste. Sprinkle with herbs. Let stand, covered, for 2 minutes before serving.

Micro-Tips

Tips for microwaving fresh vegetables

• The speed of the microwave works best with smaller batches. If you want to double this recipe, for example, to serve a crowd, microwave in two batches rather than attempting to double the quantity.

• Uniformly cut vegetables will cook more evenly than irregular cut ones.

• As a general guideline when microwaving vegetables, such as broccoli, cauliflower and carrots, add 1 tbsp (15 mL) water or stock for each cup (250 mL) of vegetables.

• Fresh-picked garden vegetables have a higher moisture content and cook more quickly than vegetables stored for a period of time.

• Refrigerated vegetables also take longer to cook than those at room temperature.

• Salt vegetables only after cooking as salt can toughen vegetables.

• Microwave vegetables until barely tender as they continue to cook once out of the oven.

Honey Acorn Squash

I am convinced more people would eat squash if it didn't take so long to cook. That's where the speed of the microwave comes to the rescue. Tasty squash that takes an hour or more to bake in the oven only needs 15 minutes in the microwave.

10-cup (2.5 L) shallow rectangular baking dish with lid

1	acorn squash (2 lbs/1 kg)	1
1 to 2 tbsp	butter	15 to 25 mL
1 tbsp	packed brown sugar	15 mL
	Salt and freshly ground black pepper	

1. Cut squash lengthwise in half. Remove seeds from center cavity. Place both halves, cut side up, in baking dish and cover with lid or plastic wrap with one corner turned back to vent.

2. Microwave on High for 10 to 14 minutes, turning dish halfway through cooking, until squash is tender when pierced with a fork. Let stand, covered, for 5 minutes.

3. Combine butter and brown sugar in a small glass measure. Microwave, uncovered, on High for 30 to 45 seconds. Brush or drizzle over squash cavities. Or scoop flesh of squash into a bowl and mash. Add butter mixture. Season with salt and pepper to taste.

Making Squash or Pumpkin Purée

With a microwave, it's so easy to enjoy nutritious winter squash, it cooks in just a fraction of the time of a conventional oven.

1. Cut squash into halves or quarters and remove seeds. For large pumpkins, cut into chunks. Place in a 12-cup (3 L) casserole dish. Add $1/2$ cup (125 mL) water. Microwave, covered, on High for 15 to 30 minutes or until squash is tender when tested with a knife in several places. Cooking time will vary according to the amount and type of squash or pumpkin. Let stand for 10 minutes or until cool enough to handle. Scoop out pulp and mash or purée in a blender or food processor.

2. Squash and pumpkin tend to be very watery, so place purée in fine-meshed strainer to drain excess moisture. Freeze in containers for up to 3 months.

Couscous Salad with Orange and Basil

I always keep couscous in my cupboard for quick-fix salads and side dishes. Here's a tasty salad that's an ideal accompaniment with grilled lamb chops or patties.

Variation

Couscous Salad with Cumin and Cilantro: Use chopped cilantro instead of basil and add 1 tsp (5 mL) ground cumin.

8-cup (2 L) casserole dish with lid

1 1/4 cups	chicken stock	300 mL
1/4 cup	raisins	50 mL
1/4 cup	chopped dried apricots	50 mL
1 cup	regular or whole wheat couscous	250 mL
1	small red bell pepper, finely diced	1
3	green onions, sliced	3
1/4 cup	slivered unblanched almonds, lightly toasted (see Micro-Tip, below)	50 mL
1/4 cup	chopped fresh basil or parsley	50 mL
3 tbsp	olive oil	45 mL
1 tsp	finely grated orange zest	5 mL
2 tbsp	freshly squeezed orange juice	25 mL
1 tsp	granulated sugar	5 mL
	Salt and freshly ground black pepper	

1. In casserole dish, combine stock, raisins and apricots. Microwave, covered, on High for 3 to 5 or until liquid comes to a full boil. Stir in couscous.

2. Cover and let stand for 5 minutes. Fluff with a fork to break up any lumps. Uncover and let cool to room temperature. Stir in red pepper, green onions, almonds and basil.

3. In a small bowl, combine oil, orange zest and juice and sugar. Season with salt and pepper to taste. Pour over salad and toss to coat well. Serve at room temperature.

Micro-Tip

To toast almonds: Spread evenly in a 9-inch (23 cm) microwave-safe pie plate. Microwave on High for 2 1/2 to 4 minutes, stirring every 30 seconds, until golden. (Watch carefully to prevent burning.)

Creamy
Green Bean Salad

For a main-course salad, add thin strips of smoked ham or barbecued chicken bought from your supermarket's deli counter. Other fresh herbs such as basil or chives can replace the dill.

8-cup (2 L) casserole dish with lid

| 1 lb | green beans, ends trimmed and halved | 500 g |
| ½ | small red onion, thinly sliced | ½ |

DRESSING

⅓ cup	sour cream	75 mL
2 tbsp	red wine vinegar	25 mL
1 tbsp	Dijon mustard	15 mL
1 tbsp	liquid honey	15 mL
2 tbsp	chopped fresh dill	25 mL
	Salt and freshly ground black pepper	

1. In casserole dish, combine beans and ½ cup (125 mL) water. Microwave, covered, on High for 5 to 8 minutes or until beans are bright green and crisp. Rinse under cold water to chill and drain well. Blot dry with paper towels. Place beans and red onion in a serving bowl.

2. *Dressing:* In a small bowl, whisk together sour cream, vinegar, mustard, honey and dill. Pour over bean mixture and toss to coat well. Season with salt and pepper to taste. Refrigerate until serving time. (Can be refrigerated for up to 1 day ahead.)

Potato Dill Salad

For an easy supper, just add cold cuts to this tasty salad. You can also add slices of knackwurst or ham cubes for a main-course salad.

8-cup (2 L) casserole dish with lid

1½ lbs	large new potatoes (about 4)	750 g
½ tsp	salt	2 mL
⅔ cup	diced dill pickles	150 mL
2	stalks celery, chopped	2
3	green onions, sliced	3
½ cup	sour cream	125 mL
⅓ cup	light mayonnaise	75 mL
1 tbsp	Dijon mustard	15 mL
2 tbsp	chopped fresh dill or parsley	25 mL
	Salt and freshly ground black pepper	

1. Peel potatoes, if desired. Cut into ½-inch (1 cm) cubes. Place in casserole dish with ½ cup (125 mL) water and salt. Microwave, covered, on High for 8 to 12 minutes, stirring once, until just tender. Drain potatoes in a sieve and quickly rinse under cold water. Drain well and let cool.

2. In a serving bowl, combine potatoes, pickles, celery and green onions.

3. In another bowl, combine sour cream, mayonnaise and mustard. Pour over potato mixture and toss gently. Add dill. Toss well. Season with salt and pepper to taste. Refrigerate until serving time.

Warm Potato Salad with Goat Cheese and Walnuts

Serves 4 to 6

Potatoes can always be counted on as the classic salad favorite for barbecues and summertime entertaining. Instead of the typical mayonnaise dressing, give new potatoes a sophisticated spin with goat cheese and walnuts.

Tip

I prefer Californian walnuts for best flavor. To toast walnuts, spread on baking sheet and toast in preheated 350°F (180°C) oven for 7 to 9 minutes or until fragrant. Rub warm nuts in clean dry kitchen towel to remove skins, then chop.

Variation

Substitute feta cheese for the goat cheese and chopped fresh oregano for the basil, if desired.

8-cup (2 L) casserole dish with lid

1½ lbs	small new potatoes, halved or quartered	750 g
½ tsp	salt	2 mL
1	large red bell pepper, diced	1
½ cup	toasted walnuts, coarsely chopped (see Tip, left)	125 mL
2 tbsp	chopped fresh basil	25 mL
2 tbsp	chopped fresh chives	25 mL
¼ cup	olive oil	50 mL
2 tbsp	red wine vinegar	25 mL
	Freshly ground black pepper	
4 oz	goat cheese, crumbled	125 g

1. In casserole dish, combine potatoes with ½ cup (125 mL) water and salt. Microwave, covered, on High for 7 to 10 minutes, stirring once, until just tender. Drain in sieve and quickly rinse under cold water. Drain well.

2. In a serving bowl, combine warm potatoes, red pepper, walnuts, basil and chives.

3. In a small bowl, whisk together oil and vinegar. Pour over potato mixture. Season with pepper to taste. Toss gently. Sprinkle with goat cheese and toss again. Serve salad warm or at room temperature.

Curried Basmati Rice and Apple Salad

Crunchy apples and radishes combined with chutney and curry make a refreshing summertime salad. If you have some almonds on hand, toast in a skillet and add them, too.

Tip

Basmati rice should always be rinsed first before cooking. It also benefits from soaking, covered, in cold water for 10 minutes resulting in long separate grains when cooked.

8-cup (2 L) casserole dish with lid

1 cup	basmati rice (see Tip, left)	250 mL
1/2 tsp	salt	2 mL
1	Granny Smith apple, cored and diced	1
3/4 cup	sliced radishes	175 mL
4	green onions, sliced	4
1/3 cup	raisins	75 mL
2 tbsp	vegetable oil	25 mL
2 tbsp	rice or cider vinegar	25 mL
2 tbsp	mango chutney	25 mL
2 tsp	mild curry paste or powder	10 mL
1/4 cup	chopped fresh cilantro or parsley	50 mL

1. Rinse rice under cold water and drain. In casserole dish, combine rice, $1\frac{1}{2}$ cups (375 mL) water and salt. Microwave, covered, on High for $3\frac{1}{2}$ to 5 minutes or until water comes to a full boil. Reduce to Medium (50%) for 8 to 10 minutes or until all liquid is absorbed. Let stand, covered, for 5 minutes. Fluff with fork and let rice cool to room temperature.

2. In a serving bowl, combine rice, apple, radishes, onions and raisins.

3. In a bowl, whisk together oil, vinegar, chutney and curry paste. Pour over rice and toss well. Sprinkle with cilantro. Serve at room temperature or chilled. (Can be refrigerated up to 1 day ahead.)

Warm Zucchini Salad with Parmesan

Serves 4

Serves 4

Zucchini gets a flavor lift in this warm salad to serve as a side dish at any time of the year.

8-cup (2 L) casserole dish with lid

3	zucchini (1 lb/500 g)	3
1 tsp	dried oregano leaves	5 mL
2 tbsp	olive oil	25 mL
1 tbsp	freshly squeezed lemon juice	15 mL
1½ tsp	Dijon mustard	7 mL
	Salt and freshly ground black pepper	
¼ cup	freshly grated Parmesan cheese	50 mL
2 tbsp	chopped fresh parsley	25 mL

1. Trim zucchini and cut into 2-by-¼-inch (5 by 0.5 cm) thin strips. Place in a casserole dish and sprinkle with oregano. Microwave, covered, on High for 2½ to 4 minutes, stirring once, until barely tender-crisp.

2. In a small bowl, whisk together oil, lemon juice and mustard. Season with salt and pepper to taste.

3. Drain zucchini well. Pour vinaigrette over top and toss gently. Sprinkle with Parmesan and parsley. Serve warm or at room temperature.

Micro-Tip

While most vegetables benefit from a bit of added water or stock, zucchini has so much natural moisture that it's not necessary to add any additional liquids when micro-cooking.

Asparagus Salad with Gorgonzola

Serves 4

Springtime calls for light warm salads for casual weekend entertaining.

Tips

Pine nuts do not toast well in the microwave because of their high fat content. To toast, place pine nuts in a small dry skillet over medium heat for 2 to 3 minutes, shaking pan frequently to prevent them from burning.

Try this vinaigrette with lightly steamed broccoli or beans.

Use any type of blue cheese, such as Roquefort or Danish blue.

10-cup (2.5 L) shallow rectangular baking dish or 11-by 7-inch (2 L) baking dish

1 lb	asparagus	500 g
3 tbsp	olive oil	45 mL
1 1/2 tbsp	balsamic vinegar	22 mL
	Salt and freshly ground black pepper	
2 tbsp	pine nuts, lightly toasted (see Tips, left)	25 mL
2 tbsp	chopped fresh herbs such as basil, chives or parsley	25 mL
3 oz	Gorgonzola or goat cheese, cut into pieces (see Tips, left)	90 g

1. Snap off the woody ends of asparagus. Peel ends of larger stalks, if desired. (This step is not necessary with young, tender asparagus.)

2. In baking dish, arrange asparagus spears with tips pointing toward the center. Add 1/4 cup (50 mL) water. Cover dish with lid or plastic wrap with one corner turned back to vent. Microwave on High for 3 to 5 minutes (time will vary according to thickness and size of stalks). Asparagus spears should be tender-crisp but retain their vibrant green color. Drain and place on serving plate.

3. In a bowl, whisk together oil and vinegar. Season with salt and pepper to taste. Drizzle vinaigrette over warm asparagus. Sprinkle with pine nuts, herbs and cheese. Serve warm or at room temperature.

Warm Snow Pea and Red Pepper Salad

Here's a simple way to dress up steamed vegetables. Try it with baby bok choy, broccoli or zucchini — just about any vegetables tastes wonderful in this Asian dressing.

9-inch (23 cm) microwave-safe pie plate

1 tbsp	sesame seeds	15 mL
2 tsp	toasted sesame oil	10 mL
1 tbsp	rice wine vinegar	15 mL
1 tbsp	soy sauce	15 mL
1 tsp	Dijon mustard	5 mL
Pinch	granulated sugar	Pinch
2 cups	snow peas, ends trimmed (7 oz/210 g)	500 mL
1	large red bell pepper, cut into thin 1½-inch (4 cm) strips	1

1. In a small glass measure, combine sesame seeds and sesame oil. Microwave, uncovered, on High for 1 to 2 minutes or until sesame seeds are lightly toasted. Let cool slightly. Stir in vinegar, soy sauce, mustard and sugar until smooth.

2. Rinse snow peas under cold water, shaking off excess. Arrange around outside of pie plate with red pepper strips in center. Cover with lid, inverted dinner plate or plastic wrap with one corner turned back to vent.

3. Microwave on High for 1½ to 2½ minutes or until vegetables are crisp and bright-colored. Drain well and toss with sesame vinaigrette. Serve warm or at room temperature.

Sauces
(Savory and Sweet)

Hot! Barbecue Sauce

**Makes
2 cups (500 mL)**

To make your summer cooking easy, this robust sauce is great to have on hand to perk up barbecued meats and chicken. For a tame version, reduce the hot pepper flakes or just add a splash of your favorite hot sauce at the end of cooking. Use this sauce to baste ribs, steaks and burgers.

4-cup (1 L) casserole dish with lid

1	small onion, finely chopped	1
2	large cloves garlic, minced	2
1 tbsp	vegetable oil	15 mL
1½ cups	ketchup	375 mL
¼ cup	Worcestershire sauce	50 mL
¼ cup	packed brown sugar	50 mL
2 tbsp	cider vinegar	25 mL
1½ tsp	dry mustard	7 mL
2 tsp	chili powder	10 mL
½ tsp	ground cumin	2 mL
1 tsp	hot pepper flakes or to taste	5 mL

1. In casserole dish, combine onion, garlic and oil. Microwave, covered, on High for 2 to 3 minutes or until onion is tender.

2. Add ketchup, Worcestershire sauce, sugar, vinegar, mustard, chili powder, cumin and hot pepper flakes. Microwave, covered, on High for 4 to 6 minutes, stirring once, until boiling and flavors blend. Let cool. Store sauce in a covered container in the refrigerator for up to 1 month.

Microwaving Meats and Poultry for the BBQ

■ There's no match to the wonderful flavor and aroma of a backyard barbecue. For meals in a hurry, use your microwave to cut down on the time it takes to barbecue meats and poultry.

Chicken

To partially cook chicken pieces, such as legs, thighs and bone-in breasts, in the microwave, place pieces in a shallow baking dish with thicker pieces positioned toward outside of dish. Cover with lid or parchment or waxed paper. Microwave on Medium-High (70%) for 4 to 5 minutes per lb (9 to 12 minutes per kg) rearranging once, until partially cooked.

Brush chicken lightly with oil and place on greased grill over medium-high heat, brushing occasionally with your favorite sauce, for about 15 minutes, turning occasionally, until no longer pink inside.

Spareribs

To precook spareribs in the microwave: see Spareribs with Orange Soy Sauce, page 82.

Hamburgers

To enjoy the flavor of barbecued hamburgers on a rainy day: Prepare your favorite beef, chicken or pork patties and grill over medium-high heat, basting with your favorite barbecue sauce, until no longer pink.

Remove patties from grill and let cool slightly. Wrap in plastic wrap, then place in covered container or freezer bag and freeze.

Unwrap frozen patties and place on a roasting rack or plate. Brush, if desired, with additional barbecue sauce and cover loosely with parchment or waxed paper. Microwave on Medium (50%) until heated through.

Curry Peach Basting Sauce

This tart-sweet barbecue baste is terrific to brush on chicken, lamb chops or pork ribs when grilling.

Tip

Generally, barbecue sauces and bastes that contain sugar (this includes honey, jam and ketchup) cause foods to burn and should not be brushed on until the last 10 to 15 minutes of grilling. Sauces without sugar can be applied right at the start of grilling to keep foods moist.

2-cup (500 mL) glass measure or microwave-safe glass bowl

¾ cup	peach jam	175 mL
3 tbsp	soy sauce	45 mL
3 tbsp	rice or red wine vinegar	45 mL
2	cloves garlic, minced	2
1 tbsp	mild curry paste or powder	15 mL

1. In glass measure, combine jam, soy sauce, vinegar, garlic and curry paste. Microwave, uncovered, on High for $1\frac{1}{2}$ to 2 minutes or until sauce comes to a boil. Let cool.

2. Store sauce in a covered glass jar in the refrigerator for up to 1 month.

Sweet-and-Sour Dipping Sauce

Commercial bottled sauces are convenient to use but tend to be expensive. Here's one that is not only easy on the budget but also a snap to make. It's great as a barbecue baste for chicken or pork, or as a dipping sauce for wings, chicken nuggets or appetizer egg rolls.

Tip

For a spicier kick, increase the amount of chili paste, or use chili oil or your favorite hot pepper sauce instead.

4-cup (1 L) glass measure or casserole dish

1 tbsp	cornstarch	15 mL
½ cup	orange juice	125 mL
⅓ cup	ketchup	75 mL
¼ cup	soy sauce	50 mL
2 tbsp	rice vinegar	25 mL
2 tbsp	packed brown sugar	25 mL
1 tbsp	minced fresh gingerroot	15 mL
1 tsp	Asian chili paste (optional)	5 mL

1. In glass measure, blend together cornstarch and orange juice until smooth. Stir in ketchup, soy sauce, rice vinegar, brown sugar, ginger and chili paste, if using.

2. Microwave, uncovered, on High for 3 to 4 minutes, stirring once, until sauce boils and thickens. Store sauce in a covered container in the refrigerator for up to 2 weeks.

Satay Peanut Sauce

**Makes
1 cup (250 mL)**

Serve this addictive peanut sauce with grilled beef, chicken or pork skewers or with Asian hors d'oeuvres, such as dumplings and spring rolls, and watch it disappear!

Tip

To make satay, marinate about 1 1/4 lbs (625 g) boneless beef, chicken or pork, cut into thin strips or cubes, in a mixture of 1/4 cup (50 mL) soy sauce, 2 tbsp (25 mL) vegetable oil and 2 cloves garlic, minced. Refrigerate for at least 1 hour or overnight, stirring occasionally. Thread meat onto wooden bamboo skewers that have been soaked in water for 30 minutes (this prevents the wood from charring when you barbecue). Barbecue skewers on a hot preheated grill and accompany with this pungent sauce.

4-cup (1 L) casserole dish with lid

1 tbsp	vegetable oil	15 mL
1/2	small onion, finely chopped	1/2
2	cloves garlic, minced	2
1 tbsp	minced fresh gingerroot	15 mL
1/4 tsp	hot pepper flakes	1 mL
1/3 cup	smooth peanut butter	75 mL
2 tbsp	soy sauce	25 mL
1 tbsp	freshly squeezed lime or lemon juice	15 mL
1 tbsp	packed brown sugar	15 mL

1. In casserole dish, combine oil, onion, garlic, ginger and hot pepper flakes. Microwave, covered, on High for 2 to 3 minutes or until tender.

2. Whisk in 1/2 cup (125 mL) water, peanut butter, soy sauce, lime juice and sugar. Microwave, uncovered, on High for 2 to 3 minutes, stirring once, until sauce boils.

3. Let sauce cool. Thin with additional water, if necessary. Store sauce in a covered container in the refrigerator for up to 1 month.

Cranapple Sauce

Makes
3 cups (750 mL)

■ This wonderful, easy-to-make sauce makes a tangy accompaniment to turkey, duck or pork.

8-cup (2 L) casserole dish with lid

1	bag (12 oz/375 g) cranberries, rinsed (about 3 cups/750 mL)	1
1	large Granny Smith apple, peeled, cored and diced	1
½ cup	chopped dried apricots or golden raisins	125 mL
1 cup	granulated sugar	250 mL
1 cup	apple juice	250 mL
1	large cinnamon stick, broken into 2 pieces	1
2 tsp	grated lemon zest	10 mL

1. In casserole dish, combine cranberries, apples, apricots, sugar, apple juice and cinnamon stick. Microwave, covered, on High for 7 to 10 minutes, stirring once, until mixture comes to a full boil and cranberries burst.

2. Remove cinnamon stick. Stir in lemon zest. Ladle into jars and refrigerate for up to 1 month or freeze.

Maple Rum Sauce

**Makes
2 cups (500 mL)**

Use this delectable sauce with steamed puddings and gingerbread, or over ice cream.

Tip

If you wish to omit the rum or brandy, replace it with additional maple-flavored pancake syrup.

4-cup (1 L) glass measure or casserole dish

2/3 cup	packed brown sugar	150 mL
2/3 cup	maple-flavored pancake syrup or pure maple syrup	150 mL
2 tbsp	cornstarch	25 mL
1/4 cup	dark rum or brandy (see Tip, left)	50 mL
2 tbsp	butter	25 mL

1. In glass measure, combine $3/4$ cup (175 mL) water, brown sugar and maple-flavored syrup. Blend in cornstarch until smooth.

2. Microwave, uncovered, on High for 4 to 6 minutes, stirring once, until sauce comes to a full boil and thickens.

3. Stir in rum and butter until melted. Let cool. Place in covered container and refrigerate until ready to use. Store for up to 1 week.

Micro-Tip

For smaller quantities, halve the recipe and microwave on High for $2^1/_2$ to 4 minutes or until sauce boils and thickens.

Raspberry Sauce

Makes about 1½ cups (375 mL)

Serve this luscious berry sauce drizzled over premium vanilla ice cream and fresh fruit slices, such as peach and mango, or over poached pear halves topped with a dollop of whipped cream.

Tip

Sauce can be kept in a covered jar in the refrigerator for up to 2 weeks.

4-cup (1 L) glass measure

1	package (10 oz/300 g) frozen unsweetened raspberries	1
½ cup	raspberry, red currant or apple jelly	125 mL
2 tbsp	granulated sugar	25 mL
2 tsp	cornstarch	10 mL
1 tbsp	Kirsch or raspberry-flavored liqueur (optional)	15 mL

1. In glass measure, combine frozen raspberries, jelly and sugar. Microwave, uncovered, on High for 4 to 6 minutes, stirring once, until mixture is piping hot. Using a rubber spatula, press sauce through a fine sieve into a bowl to remove seeds. Return sauce to glass measure.

2. In a small bowl, blend cornstarch with 1 tsp (5 mL) cold water until smooth. Stir into raspberry sauce and microwave, uncovered, on High for 2 to 3 minutes, stirring once, until mixture boils and thickens. Let cool. Stir in Kirsch, if desired. Refrigerate until ready to use.

Vanilla Custard Sauce

Here's an all-purpose dessert sauce to dress up a bowl of fresh fruit salad. Or pour it over a fruit crisp or slices of angel food or pound cake surrounded by berries. Another suggestion is to spread the creamy sauce on a dessert plate. Then place small scoops of double chocolate ice cream on top of sauce and surround with strawberries or raspberries for a simply, stunning dessert.

Variation

Instead of vanilla, add 2 tbsp (25 mL) orange-flavored liqueur or brandy.

4-cup (1 L) glass measure

⅓ cup	granulated sugar	75 mL
1 tbsp	cornstarch	15 mL
1 cup	milk	250 mL
1	egg yolk	1
2 tsp	vanilla	10 mL
½ cup	whipping (35%) cream	125 mL

1. In glass measure, stir together sugar and cornstarch. Blend in milk until smooth. Microwave, uncovered, on High for $2\frac{1}{2}$ to 4 minutes, whisking once, until sauce come to a full rolling boil and thickens.

2. In a bowl, beat egg yolk. Gradually whisk in about $\frac{1}{4}$ cup (50 mL) of the hot milk mixture in a thin steady stream. Gradually whisk egg mixture into hot milk mixture, stirring until blended.

3. Microwave, uncovered, on Medium (50%) for 45 to 90 seconds or until sauce bubbles around edges. Stir in vanilla. Let cool slightly. Cover surface with plastic wrap and let cool slightly, then refrigerate.

4. In a mixer bowl, using an electric mixer, whip cream until soft peaks form. Fold cream into chilled custard until sauce is smooth. Refrigerate again until ready to serve. Can be made up to 1 day ahead.

Micro-Tip

When microwaving sugar mixtures and sauces especially those containing milk or cream, always use a glass measure or bowl at least three times the volume of the liquids to prevent boil-overs.

Peanut Butter Fudge Sauce

Top your favorite ice cream with banana slices, then pour this warm sauce over top and sprinkle with roasted unsalted peanuts. It's also terrific to use when making milkshakes.

4-cup (1 L) glass measure

³⁄₄ cup	semisweet chocolate chips	175 mL
¹⁄₂ cup	smooth peanut butter	125 mL
1 cup	light (5%) cream	250 mL
¹⁄₂ cup	confectioner's (icing) sugar	125 mL
1 tsp	vanilla	5 mL

1. In glass measure, combine chocolate chips and peanut butter. Microwave, uncovered, on Medium (50%) for 2 to 3 minutes, stirring once, until chocolate melts.

2. Stir in cream, icing sugar and vanilla. Microwave, uncovered, on Medium (50%) for 1 to 1¹⁄₂ minutes until warm. Let cool. Place in covered container and refrigerate for up to 2 weeks.

Micro-Tip

Sauce thickens when refrigerated. Microwave on High for 15 to 30 seconds or until desired consistency to serve.

Maple Walnut Sauce

**Makes
2 cups (500 mL)**

For a cool summertime treat, indulge in ice cream sundaes drizzled with homemade sauce made in the microwave oven. For an adult version, add a splash of dark rum or brandy. Californian walnuts are the best choice in this recipe.

8-cup (2 L) glass measure

1 tbsp	cornstarch	15 mL
1 cup	maple-flavored pancake syrup or pure maple syrup	250 mL
½ cup	whipping (35%) cream	125 mL
½ cup	chopped walnuts	125 mL

1. In glass measure, blend cornstarch with 1 tbsp (15 mL) cold water until smooth. Stir in syrup and cream. Microwave, uncovered, on High for 3 to 4 minutes, stirring once, until sauce comes to a full rolling boil and thickens.

2. Stir in walnuts. Let cool. Place in covered container and refrigerate for up to 1 week.

Micro-Tip

If ice cream is too firm to scoop, soften first in your microwave oven. For an 8-cup (2 L) container, microwave on Low (10%) or Medium-Low (30%), for 1 to 1½ minutes, checking every 30 seconds.

Chocolate Pudding Cake (page 172)

Rhubarb Orange Sauce

Serve this tangy dessert sauce over slices of pound cake or gingerbread, or over ice cream. Vary the flavor by substituting strawberries or raspberries for part of the rhubarb called for in the recipe. The amount of sugar you use will depend on whether you prefer the rhubarb sauce on the tart or sweet side.

Variation

Rhubarb Ginger Sauce: Substitute 3 tbsp (45 mL) finely chopped crystallized ginger for the orange zest.

8-cup (2 L) casserole dish with lid

4 cups	chopped fresh or frozen rhubarb	1 L
2/3 cup	granulated sugar or to taste	150 mL
2 tsp	grated orange zest	10 mL
1/2 cup	freshly squeezed orange juice	125 mL
1 tbsp	cornstarch	15 mL

1. In casserole dish, combine rhubarb, sugar, orange zest and juice. Microwave, covered, on High for 5 to 8 minutes, stirring once, until rhubarb is tender. (If using frozen rhubarb, microwave for 9 to 13 minutes.)

2. In small bowl, blend cornstarch with 1 tbsp (15 mL) cold water until smooth. Stir into rhubarb mixture. Microwave, uncovered, on High for 3 to 4 minutes, stirring once, until sauce thickens. Let cool. Place in a covered container and refrigerate for up to 1 week.

Micro-Tip

To Stew Rhubarb: Cut 1 lb (500 g) washed and trimmed rhubarb stalks into 3/4-inch (2 cm) pieces (about 4 cups/1 L). Place in an 8-cup (2 L) casserole dish. Microwave, covered, on High for 5 to 8 minutes, stirring once, until tender. Stir in 1/2 cup (125 mL) granulated sugar or sweeten to taste. Let cool, cover and refrigerate. Stewed rhubarb also freezes well in a covered container for up to 2 months. Makes about 2 1/2 cups (625 mL) sauce.

Steamed Cranberry Orange Pudding (page 174) with Maple Rum Sauce (page 156)

Lemon Curd

Makes 1⅓ cups (325 mL)

■ This all-purpose dessert sauce can be used as filling for tart shells or as cake filling.

4-cup (1 L) glass measure

¼ cup	butter	50 mL
¾ cup	granulated sugar	175 mL
2 tsp	finely grated lemon zest	10 mL
2	eggs	2
¼ cup	freshly squeezed lemon juice	50 mL

1. In glass measure, melt butter, uncovered, on High for 30 to 45 seconds. Stir in sugar and lemon zest.

2. In another bowl, beat together eggs and lemon juice. Strain through a fine sieve into sugar mixture.

3. Microwave, uncovered, on High for 1 minute. Whisk mixture lightly. Reduce to Medium (50%) and continue to microwave, uncovered, for 1½ to 2½ minutes, whisking every 30 seconds, until lemon curd is thickened.

4. Let cool. Place in covered jar or container and store in the refrigerator for up to 2 weeks. (Curd thickens as it cools.)

Micro-Tip

■ To get more juice out of a lemon, orange or lime, microwave fruit on High for 20 to 40 seconds for one fruit and 40 to 60 seconds for two, or until slightly warm to the touch. (Increase time slightly if fruit has been refrigerated.) Roll fruit on counter using your palm and squeeze.

Desserts

Raspberry Pear Trifle with Chocolate

Pears are available year-round in supermarkets, but I find the best time to enjoy them is in the fall, when full-flavored fruit is in abundant supply. Pears poached with honey and served in a trifle make for a great do-ahead dessert.

Variations

Poached Ginger Pear Slices: Microwave sliced pears with honey as directed in recipe, adding 1 tbsp (15 mL) lemon juice and 2 tbsp (25 mL) finely chopped crystallized ginger, until just tender. Stir in 1 tsp (5 mL) grated lemon zest. Serve pears with syrup over gingerbread or ice cream.

Instead of pears, substitute 6 peaches, peeled and sliced.

8-cup (2 L) casserole dish with lid
10-cup (2.5 L) glass serving bowl

4	firm but ripe Bartlett pears, cored, peeled and sliced	4
¼ cup	liquid honey	50 mL
1½ cups	whipping (35%) cream	375 mL
⅓ cup	confectioner's (icing) sugar	75 mL
½ cup	cream cheese (4 oz/125 g), cubed	125 mL
1 tbsp	finely grated lemon zest	15 mL
1	frozen pound cake (10 oz/300 g), cut into ¾-inch (2 cm) cubes	1
	Raspberry Sauce (see recipe, page 157)	
2 oz	semisweet chocolate (2 squares), grated	60 g

1. In casserole dish, combine pears and honey. Microwave, covered, on High for 4 to 6 minutes or until pears are just barely tender. Let cool. Refrigerate for 2 hours or until chilled.

2. In a mixer bowl, using an electric mixer, beat cream until soft peaks form. Add confectioner's sugar and continue to beat until stiff. Set aside 1 cup (250 mL) whipped cream to frost top.

3. In a glass bowl, microwave cream cheese, uncovered, on Medium (50%) for 30 to 45 seconds or until softened. Whisk in 2 tbsp (25 mL) pear poaching juice and lemon zest until smooth. Fold in whipped cream.

4. To assemble, place half of the cake cubes in bottom of serving bowl. Top with half of the pear slices, including juice. Drizzle with half of the raspberry sauce. Spread with half of the cream cheese mixture.

5. Layer with remaining cake cubes, pear slices with juice, raspberry sauce and cream cheese mixture. Spread with reserved whipped cream and sprinkle with grated chocolate. Cover and refrigerate for 4 hours until chilled or overnight. (Trifle can be make up to 1 day ahead.)

Strawberry Mousse Pie

Serves 6 to 8

This heavenly combination of chocolate and strawberries disappears quickly when I serve it to a crowd.

Tip

Chocolate wafer crumbs are also referred to as chocolate baking crumbs or Oreo baking crumbs in supermarkets. If unavailable, substitute graham wafer crumbs instead.

9-inch (23 cm) microwave-safe pie plate

CRUST

¼ cup	butter	50 mL
1¼ cups	chocolate wafer crumbs (see Tip, left)	300 mL
2 tbsp	granulated sugar	25 mL

FILLING

2 tbsp	freshly squeezed lime juice	25 mL
1	packet (¼ oz/7.5 g) powdered unflavored gelatin	1
3 cups	sliced strawberries, divided	750 mL
¾ cup	granulated sugar	175 mL
½ cup	strawberry-flavored yogurt	125 mL
½ cup	whipping (35%) cream, whipped	125 mL
	Whipped cream for garnish (optional)	

1. *Crust:* In a bowl, melt butter, uncovered, on High for 45 to 60 seconds. Stir in chocolate crumbs and sugar. Press crumbs evenly in bottom and up sides of glass pie plate to form a shell. Microwave, uncovered, on Medium-High (70%) for 2 to 3 minutes, rotating dish once, until just set. Let cool.

2. *Filling:* In a bowl, combine lime juice and 2 tbsp (25 mL) water. Sprinkle gelatin over top. Let stand for 1 minute to soften. Microwave, uncovered, on Medium (50%) for 40 to 60 seconds or until gelatin is dissolved. Let cool slightly.

3. In a food processor or blender, purée 2 cups (500 mL) strawberries and sugar. Transfer to a bowl. Stir in yogurt and dissolved gelatin mixture. Refrigerate for 30 to 45 minutes, stirring occasionally, until mixture just starts to thicken.

4. Fold whipped cream into strawberry mixture. Pour into pie shell and refrigerate until set, about 2 hours. To serve, garnish with remaining sliced strawberries and whipped cream, if desired.

Lemon Cheesecake Mousse with Strawberries

Classic mousse — the airy but light whipped cream concoction — is still one of simplest and most elegant desserts to end a special meal. This version, with the subtle essence of lemon, mimics a cheesecake.

4-cup (1 L) glass measure

1	packet (¼ oz/7.5 g) powdered unflavored gelatin	1
¾ cup	frozen lemonade concentrate, defrosted, undiluted	175 mL
⅓ cup	granulated sugar	75 mL
1	package (8 oz/250 g) light cream cheese, cubed	1
½ cup	plain yogurt	125 mL
1½ tsp	finely grated lemon zest	7 mL
1 cup	whipping (35%) cream	250 mL

TOPPING

3 cups	sliced fresh strawberries	750 mL
2 tbsp	granulated sugar or to taste	25 mL

1. In glass measure, sprinkle gelatin over ¼ cup (50 mL) cold water and let stand for 1 minute to soften. Add undiluted lemonade concentrate and sugar. Microwave, uncovered, on High for 2 to 3 minutes, stirring once, until mixture is hot and sugar dissolves. Let cool slightly, then refrigerate for 45 to 60 minutes or until the consistency of egg whites.

2. In a bowl, microwave cream cheese, uncovered, on Medium (50%) for 1 to 1½ minutes or until softened. Whisk in yogurt and lemon zest until smooth. Stir in gelatin mixture.

3. In a mixer bowl, using an electric mixer, whip cream until soft peaks form. Gently fold into cream cheese mixture. Divide evenly among 6 individual serving bowls. Chill until set, about 2 hours.

4. *Topping:* In a bowl, combine sliced strawberries and sugar to taste. Top mousse with berries just before serving.

Micro-Tip

Chocolate-Dipped Strawberries: Wash and dry 12 whole strawberries with hulls. Place $1/2$ cup (125 mL) semisweet chocolate chips and 1 tsp (5 mL) vegetable oil in a small glass measure. Microwave, uncovered, on Medium (50%) for $1^1/_2$ to 2 minutes, stirring once, until melted and smooth. Let cool for 10 minutes. Holding by the stem end, dip each berry in the chocolate, twirling to cover two-thirds of the berry. Place on waxed paper–lined baking sheet and refrigerate for 30 minutes or until set. Also delicious with sweet dark cherries!

Bananas in Spiced Rum Sauce

By adding a splash of spirits, you can turn bananas into a special-occasion dessert in a matter of minutes using your microwave oven.

Tip

If bananas are large, use only 3 instead of the 4 called for in the recipe.

2-cup (500 mL) glass measure
8-inch (2 L) square baking dish

2 tbsp	freshly squeezed orange juice	25 mL
1 tbsp	freshly squeezed lime juice	15 mL
1/3 cup	packed brown sugar	75 mL
2 tbsp	butter	25 mL
1/4 tsp	ground cinnamon	1 mL
1/4 tsp	freshly grated nutmeg	1 mL
1/4 cup	dark rum	50 mL
4	firm but ripe bananas (see Tip, left)	4
	Frozen yogurt or ice cream	

1. In glass measure, combine orange juice, lime juice, brown sugar, butter, cinnamon and nutmeg. Microwave, uncovered, on High for 2 to 3 minutes, stirring once, until sauce boils and is reduced slightly. Add rum.

2. Peel bananas and halve lengthwise. Cut each half into 2 pieces. Arrange banana pieces in single layer in shallow baking dish and pour sauce over top. Cover loosely with waxed paper and microwave on High for 2 1/2 to 4 minutes or until bananas are softened and heated through.

3. Spoon frozen yogurt into serving dishes and top with warm bananas and sauce.

Micro-Tip

To soften hardened brown sugar: Place sugar in a bowl and top with a slice of apple or bread. Cover with vented plastic wrap and microwave on High for 30 seconds per each cup (250 mL) of sugar. Use a fork to break up lumps.

Fresh Pineapple with Citrus Sauce

■ For an easy entertaining dessert, dress up fresh pineapple with a luxurious liqueur-flavored sauce.

Tips

How to choose a perfectly ripe pineapple? Pineapples do not ripen once picked. Color is not a good indicator as the rind of a ripe pineapple can be anywhere from green to golden. The best advice is to choose a plump, fresh-looking one with green leaves and a sweet fragrance.

Most supermarkets sell fresh peeled pineapple, but if the chore of peeling pineapple is left to you, here's how: Cut off top and bottom of pineapple and stand it upright on a cutting board. Using a sharp knife, cut off thick strips of peel from top to bottom. Instead of cutting out eyes one by one, cut grooves in fruit using a sharp knife, following diagonal lines like that of a barber's pole.

4-cup (1 L) glass measure or bowl

1/3 cup	packed brown sugar	75 mL
1/3 cup	orange marmalade	75 mL
2 tsp	grated lemon zest	10 mL
1/4 cup	freshly squeezed lemon juice	50 mL
1 tbsp	minced fresh gingerroot	15 mL
1/4 cup	orange liqueur, such as Cointreau, or rum, or orange juice	50 mL
1	pineapple, cut into 1-inch (2.5 cm) chunks (6 cups/1.5 L) (see Tips, left)	1
	Frozen vanilla yogurt or lemon sorbet	

1. In glass measure, combine brown sugar, marmalade, lemon zest, lemon juice and ginger. Microwave, uncovered, on High for 1½ to 2½ minutes, stirring once, until mixture comes to a full boil and is reduced slightly. Stir in orange liqueur.

2. Place pineapple chunks in a serving bowl and pour sauce over top. Cover and refrigerate until serving time. (Can be made up to 2 days ahead.)

3. To serve, ladle fruit with sauce into dessert bowls and top with a scoop of frozen yogurt.

Brown Sugar Apple Slices with Raisins

Serves 4

This quick dessert sauce to serve over ice cream tastes just like old-fashioned apple pie, but without the effort of making pastry and baking an actual pie.

8-cup (2 L) casserole dish with lid

½ cup	packed brown sugar	125 mL
1 tbsp	cornstarch	15 mL
4	large apples, peeled, cored and sliced	4
⅓ cup	raisins	75 mL
2 tbsp	freshly squeezed lemon juice	25 mL
½ tsp	ground cinnamon	2 mL
2 tbsp	butter	25 mL
	Ice cream	

1. In casserole dish, combine brown sugar and cornstarch. Stir in apple slices, raisins, lemon juice and cinnamon. Dot with butter.

2. Microwave, covered, on High for 4 to 6 minutes, stirring once, until apples are just tender and sauce is slightly thickened.

3. Spoon over ice cream. Serve either warm or at room temperature.

Micro-Tip

Here's how to make applesauce in the microwave: Peel and core 2 lbs (1 kg) apples (about 4 to 6 apples depending on size) such as MacIntosh, Empire or Cortland. Cut into 1-inch (2.5 cm) pieces. Place in 8-cup (2 L) casserole dish and microwave, covered, on High for 8 to 12 minutes or until very soft. Mash with a fork, or purée in food processor, if desired. Sweeten with granulated sugar to taste. Makes 2 cups (500 mL).

Maple Baked Apples

Use a firm variety of cooking apple, such as Granny Smith or Golden Delicious, to make this old-time favorite dessert. Serve warm with ice cream, if desired.

8-inch (2 L) casserole dish with lid

2 tbsp	butter	25 mL
1/4 cup	packed brown sugar	50 mL
2 tbsp	dried cranberries or raisins	25 mL
2 tbsp	finely chopped pecans or walnuts	25 mL
4	cooking apples	4
1/4 cup	maple-flavored pancake syrup	50 mL
1 tsp	cornstarch	5 mL

1. In a bowl, microwave butter, uncovered, on High for 10 to 15 seconds or until softened. Blend in brown sugar, dried cranberries and pecans.

2. Core apples and peel skins two-thirds of the way down. Firmly pack the cranberry nut mixture into apple centers.

3. Arrange apples in casserole dish. Drizzle with syrup. Microwave, covered, on High for 4 1/2 to 7 minutes or until apples are just tender when pierced with a knife (be careful not to overcook). Transfer apples to individual serving bowls, leaving juices in dish.

4. In a small bowl, blend cornstarch with 2 tsp (10 mL) cold water. Stir into sauce in dish. Microwave, uncovered, on High for 1 to 1 1/2 minutes until sauce boils and thickens. Pour over apples and serve.

Micro-Tip

To plump dried fruit such as raisins in the microwave: Rinse under water, shake off excess and place on a paper towel–lined plate. For 1/2 cup (125 mL) fruit, microwave, uncovered, on High for 30 to 45 seconds. Allow additional time for larger quantities.

Chocolate Pudding Cake

Here's a warm dessert with a fudgy cake layer on the top and a rich chocolate sauce on the bottom that's a treat for kids and grown-ups alike.

Tips

Pudding can also be baked in a preheated 350°F (180°C) oven for 30 to 35 minutes or until a cake tester inserted in center comes out clean.

Chocolate chip ice cream pairs well with this rich-tasting dessert.

8-inch (2 L) square baking dish

CHOCOLATE SAUCE

²/₃ cup	granulated sugar	150 mL
3 tbsp	unsweetened cocoa powder	45 mL
1¹/₂ cups	water	375 mL

BATTER

¹/₄ cup	butter	50 mL
¹/₂ cup	milk	125 mL
1	egg	1
1 tsp	vanilla	5 mL
1 cup	all-purpose flour	250 mL
¹/₂ cup	granulated sugar	125 mL
¹/₄ cup	unsweetened cocoa powder	50 mL
2 tsp	baking powder	10 mL
Pinch	salt	Pinch
	Ice cream (optional)	

1. *Chocolate Sauce:* In baking dish, combine sugar, cocoa powder and water. Stir until smooth. Microwave, uncovered, on High for 2¹/₂ to 4 minutes, stirring once, until sauce is very hot. Stir well.

2. *Batter:* In a glass mixing bowl, microwave butter, uncovered, on High for 40 to 60 seconds or until melted. Beat in milk, egg and vanilla.

3. In another bowl, stir together flour, sugar, cocoa powder, baking powder and salt. Stir milk mixture into flour mixture just until combined. Batter will be quite thick.

4. Drop spoonfuls of batter as evenly as possible into chocolate sauce in baking dish (do not stir together). Place an inverted dinner plate in bottom of microwave and set dish on plate. Microwave, uncovered, on Medium (50%) for 7 to 10 minutes, until top of cake has risen and only few moist spots remain.

5. Let dish stand directly on heatproof surface for 10 minutes before serving (see Micro-Tips, 177). Spoon warm dessert into dishes along with some of the sauce and serve with ice cream, if desired.

Micro-Tip

If using an older oven without a turntable, rotate dish twice during cooking so that cake topping cooks evenly.

Vanilla Pudding

Serves 4

Creamy puddings make nutritious and economical desserts that are incredibly easy to whip-up in your microwave oven.

Tips

Use whole milk to give puddings a creamier consistency.

Use a large bowl or casserole to prevent boil-overs and stir pudding often to prevent lumps from forming.

Variations

Chocolate Pudding: Whisk in 1/3 cup (75 mL) semisweet chocolate chips into hot pudding along with vanilla until melted.

Butterscotch Pudding: Substitute brown sugar for the granulated sugar.

8-cup (2 L) glass measure or casserole dish

2 cups	milk (see Tips, left)	500 mL
2	egg yolks	2
1/3 cup	granulated sugar	75 mL
3 tbsp	cornstarch	45 mL
2 tsp	vanilla	10 mL

1. In glass measure, whisk together milk and egg yolks. Stir in sugar and cornstarch until smooth.

2. Microwave, uncovered, on High for 2 minutes. Stir well with a whisk. Continue to microwave on High for 2 to 5 minutes, whisking every minute, until pudding comes to a full boil and thickens.

3. Stir in vanilla. Pour pudding into individual serving dishes. Serve pudding warm or cold. If serving cold, let cool slightly and place a piece of plastic wrap directly on surface to prevent a skin from forming.

Steamed Cranberry Orange Pudding

Serves 8

Traditional comfort foods like steamed puddings that take hours to cook in a boiling water bath can now be steamed in the microwave in a fraction of the time.

Tip

The easiest way to chop the cranberries is in your food processor.

8-cup (2 L) glass ring mold or 9-inch (23 cm) round baking dish with a 2½-inch (6 cm) heatproof glass

⅓ cup	butter	75 mL
¾ cup	packed brown sugar	175 mL
2	eggs	2
1 tbsp	grated orange zest	15 mL
⅓ cup	freshly squeezed orange juice	75 mL
1 cup	all-purpose flour	250 mL
1½ tsp	baking powder	7 mL
Pinch	salt	Pinch
2 cups	fresh or frozen cranberries, finely chopped (see Tip, left)	500 mL
¾ cup	raisins	175 mL
⅔ cup	chopped pecans or walnuts	150 mL
	Maple Rum Sauce (see recipe, page 156)	

1. If using a ring mold, line with 4 strips of parchment paper, overlapping as necessary to cover bottom of mold. Grease parchment. If using a round baking dish, line bottom with parchment paper and place the glass upside down in center to simulate a ring mold. Grease parchment and glass.

2. In a mixer bowl, using an electric mixer, cream butter and sugar. Beat in eggs, one at a time, until incorporated. Add orange zest and juice.

3. In another bowl, combine flour, baking powder and salt. Stir into creamed mixture until combined. Fold in cranberries, raisins and pecans.

4. Spoon batter evenly into prepared glass ring mold or prepared baking dish.

5. Place an inverted dinner plate in bottom of microwave and set dish on plate. Microwave, uncovered, on Medium (50%) for 6 minutes. Rotate dish, if necessary, and microwave on High for 2 to 4 minutes longer or until a toothpick inserted in center comes out clean.

6. Let dish stand directly on heatproof surface for 15 minutes (see Micro-Tips, page 177). Run a knife around the edge of dish. Invert onto serving plate and let cool completely.

7. To reheat pudding, microwave, uncovered, on Medium (50%) for 4 to 7 minutes or until warm to the touch. Serve with Maple Rum Sauce.

Micro-Tip

To reheat your favorite steamed pudding, place on a serving plate and microwave, uncovered, on Medium (50%) until warm to the touch. Time will depend on size — estimate 5 to 8 minutes for a dense pudding laden with dried fruits.

Creamy Rice Pudding

Serves 4 to 6

A traditional rice pudding like those our grandmothers used to make took long hours of baking in a conventional oven. Here's a quick, creamy version with that old-fashioned flavor. Either whole evaporated milk or the less rich 2% evaporated milk works well in this recipe.

8-cup (2 L) casserole dish with lid
8-cup (2 L) glass measure

½ cup	long-grain white rice	125 mL
1⅔ cups	water	400 mL
Pinch	salt	Pinch
½ cup	granulated sugar	125 mL
2 tbsp	cornstarch	25 mL
1	can (12 oz/385 mL) evaporated milk	1
½ cup	raisins	125 mL
2 tsp	vanilla	10 mL
	Ground cinnamon (optional)	

1. In casserole dish, combine rice, water and salt. Microwave, covered, on High for 4 to 6 minutes or until water boils. Reduce to Medium (50%) and microwave for 10 to 15 minutes longer or until rice is very tender and most of the water is absorbed. Let stand, covered, for 10 minutes or until water is completely absorbed.

2. In glass measure, blend sugar with cornstarch. Stir in evaporated milk until smooth. Microwave, uncovered, on High for 3 to 5 minutes, stirring twice, until mixture comes to a full rolling boil and thickens. Add raisins and vanilla.

3. Stir custard into hot rice. Let stand, covered, for 30 minutes before serving. (Rice will continue to thicken upon cooling.) Serve either warm or at room temperature. Sprinkle with cinnamon, if desired.

Micro-Tip

The key to a creamy rice pudding made with long-grain rice is to make sure the rice is cooked until very tender. If refrigerated, rice pudding will thicken; thin with a bit of milk to desired consistency.

Gingerbread

Serves 6

I like to serve this with a dusting of icing sugar as a snacking cake or for dessert try it with Rhubarb Orange Sauce (see recipe, page 161).

8-inch (2 L) square baking dish, lightly greased

1/4 cup	vegetable oil	50 mL
1/3 cup	fancy molasses	75 mL
1/3 cup	packed brown sugar	75 mL
1	egg	1
1 cup	grated apple (about 1 large)	250 mL
1 cup	all-purpose flour	250 mL
1/2 tsp	baking soda	2 mL
1/4 tsp	baking powder	1 mL
1 tsp	ground ginger	5 mL
1/2 tsp	ground cinnamon	2 mL

1. In a mixing bowl, combine oil, molasses, brown sugar, egg and apple.

2. In another bowl, stir together flour, baking soda, baking powder, ginger and cinnamon. Stir into molasses mixture until well combined.

3. Spread batter evenly in prepared baking dish, pushing batter into corners. Place an inverted dinner plate in bottom of microwave oven and place dish on plate. Microwave, uncovered, on High for 4 to 5 minutes, until evenly puffed and no moist spots remain on surface. Let dish stand directly on heatproof surface to cool (see Micro-Tips, below).

Micro-Tips

Baking in the Microwave: Elevate the dish by placing on an inverted dinner plate in bottom of microwave to promote even cooking.

Baked goods need to stand after cooking in the microwave to allow for "carry-over cooking." Place the dish on a solid heatproof surface that allows for heat retention, such as a wooden cutting board or heatproof countertop, rather than a wire rack, and let stand for the specified time.

The microwave does wonders with poached fruits, creamy puddings, ice cream sauces, moist chewy brownies and many quick breads such as this spiced gingerbread. But there are limits when baking flaky pie crusts, tender pastries, sponge cakes and crisp cookies — these are best baked in your conventional oven.

Nanaimo Bars

These buttery coconut concoctions were invented in Nanaimo, British Columbia — hence the name. No matter where they were invented, however, they're delicious eaten anywhere.

Tip

Traditionally 2 tbsp (25 mL) custard powder is used in the icing of Nanaimo Bars. If available in your supermarket, add custard powder to confectioner's sugar and omit vanilla.

8-cup (2 L) glass measure
9-inch (2.5 L) square baking pan, buttered or 11-by 7-inch (2 L) baking dish

BASE

½ cup	butter, cubed	125 mL
⅓ cup	unsweetened cocoa powder	75 mL
¼ cup	granulated sugar	50 mL
1	egg, beaten	1
1½ cups	graham wafer crumbs	375 mL
1 cup	sweetened desiccated coconut	250 mL
½ cup	chopped walnuts	125 mL

ICING

¼ cup	butter, softened	50 mL
2 cups	confectioner's (icing) sugar	500 mL
2 tbsp	milk	25 mL
1½ tsp	vanilla	7 mL

TOPPING

¾ cup	semisweet chocolate chips	175 mL
2 tbsp	butter	25 mL

1. *Base:* In glass measure, melt butter, uncovered, on High for 1 minute.

2. Stir in cocoa powder, sugar and egg until smooth. Microwave, uncovered, on Medium (50%) for 1½ to 2 minutes, stirring once, until slightly thickened. Stir in graham wafer crumbs, coconut and walnuts. Press mixture firmly into prepared baking pan.

3. *Icing:* In a mixer bowl, using an electric mixer, cream butter until fluffy. Stir in icing sugar, milk and vanilla until smooth. Spread evenly over base and refrigerate for 30 minutes or until firm.

4. *Topping:* In a microwave-safe bowl, combine chocolate chips and butter. Microwave, uncovered, on Medium (50%) for 2 to 3 minutes or until melted and smooth. Let cool slightly. Spread mixture over icing layer. Refrigerate until chilled and firm before cutting into squares.

Micro-Tip

To toast coconut: Spread ½ cup (125 mL) sweetened coconut evenly in 9-inch (23 cm) microwave-safe pie plate. Microwave on High for 1 to 2 minutes, stirring every 20 to 30 seconds. (Watch carefully to prevent burning.)

Chocolate Irish Cream Fondue

A colorful fruit assortment of whole strawberries, pear slices, kiwi slices, banana slices along with individual dishes of chocolate fondue makes an easy, decadent dessert that everyone will love.

Tip

Cut-up cubes of pound cake or biscotti are other suggestions to combine with the fruit selection.

4-cup (1 L) glass measure
4 custard cups or ramekins

1 cup	semisweet chocolate chips	250 mL
1/2 cup	whipping (35%) cream	125 mL
1/4 cup	Irish cream liqueur	50 mL
	Assorted fresh fruit, cut into serving-size pieces	

1. In glass measure, combine chocolate chips, cream and Irish cream liqueur. Microwave, uncovered, on Medium (50%) for 3 to 5 minutes, stirring once, until chocolate is melted and mixture is smooth.

2. Divide warm chocolate among 4 custard cups or ramekins. Place on dessert plates and surround with fruit for dipping.

Micro-Tip

For single serving — combine 1/4 cup (50 mL) semisweet chocolate chips with 2 tbsp (25 mL) whipping (35%) cream and 1 tbsp (15 mL) Irish cream liqueur. Microwave, uncovered, on Medium (50%) for 1 to 1 1/2 minutes. Stir well, until chocolate melts and is smooth.

Double Chocolate Brownies

Makes 16 squares

You'll love the moist and chewy texture of these super fast brownies that only take about five minutes to make in the microwave.

Tip

For easy cleanup and cutting brownies into squares, line baking dish with parchment or waxed paper overlapping at two ends. Refrigerate or partially freeze brownies until firm. Use parchment ends to lift out brownies and cut into perfect squares.

8-cup (2 L) glass measure
8-inch (2 L) square baking dish, lined with parchment or waxed paper

½ cup	butter	125 mL
3 oz	unsweetened chocolate (3 squares), chopped	90 g
1 cup	granulated sugar	250 mL
2	eggs	2
1½ tsp	vanilla	7 mL
1 cup	all-purpose flour	250 mL
½ tsp	baking powder	2 mL
¼ tsp	salt	1 mL
½ cup	finely chopped pecans or walnuts	125 mL
½ cup	semisweet chocolate chips	125 mL
TOPPING		
¼ cup	semisweet chocolate chips	50 mL
1 tbsp	butter	15 mL

1. In glass measure, microwave butter and chocolate, uncovered, on Medium (50%) for 2 to 3 minutes, stirring once, or until melted and smooth. Whisk in sugar until smooth. Then whisk in eggs and vanilla.

2. In another bowl, stir together flour, baking powder and salt. Stir into chocolate mixture. Fold in pecans and ½ cup (125 mL) chocolate chips. Spoon batter into baking dish, spreading into corners of dish. Place an inverted dinner plate in bottom of microwave oven and place dish on plate.

3. Microwave, uncovered, on High for 4 to 6 minutes or until top is evenly puffed and no moist spots remain on surface. Let dish stand directly on heatproof surface for 10 minutes (see Micro-Tips, page 177).

4. *Topping:* In glass bowl, combine $1/4$ cup (50 mL) chocolate chips and butter. Microwave, uncovered, on Medium (50%) for 1 to $1^1/_2$ minutes or until melted and smooth. Pour over brownies and evenly spread. Let cool completely before cutting into squares.

Micro-Tips

■ Chocolate Melting Times

To melt chocolate squares:
Unwrap chocolate and place squares in microwave-safe shallow glass bowl. When melting 3 or more squares, place in a microwave-safe pie plate spacing evenly apart and rotating dish once when melting chocolate.

Microwave, uncovered, on Medium (50%) for the following times:

1 square	1 to 2 minutes
2 squares	2 to 3 minutes
4 squares	3 to $4^1/_2$ minutes

Note: When chocolate is coarsely chopped, it will melt more quickly.

Chocolate Chips:
Place in a wide shallow bowl and microwave, uncovered, on Medium (50%), stirring once:

$1/2$ cup (125 mL)	1 to 2 minutes
1 cup (250 mL)	2 to 3 minutes

Watch carefully as chocolate can scorch if overheated.

Peanut Butter Raisin Crispies

Looking for an activity to keep kids busy? Get them cooking using the microwave oven. These crispies are a quick and easy snack recipe for kids to make and eat.

4-cup (1 L) glass measure or casserole dish
8-inch (2 L) square baking pan or dish, buttered

4 cups	crisp rice cereal	1 L
½ cup	raisins	125 mL
¾ cup	peanut butter	175 mL
½ cup	packed brown sugar	125 mL
½ cup	corn syrup	125 mL

1. In a large bowl, combine cereal and raisins.

2. In glass measure, combine peanut butter, brown sugar and corn syrup. Microwave, uncovered, on High for 2 to 3 minutes, stirring once, until mixture is smooth and comes to a full boil.

3. Pour over cereal and mix well. Press into prepared baking pan. Refrigerate until chilled and firm before cutting into squares.

Raisin Nut Popcorn Balls

Makes 12

■ Here's a tempting, popular treat for a fun activity at a child's party.

8-cup (2 L) glass measure or casserole dish

10 cups	popped corn (1 bag microwave popcorn, about 3 oz/85 g) (see Micro-Tips, below)	2.5 L
½ cup	raisins	125 mL
½ cup	salted peanuts	125 mL
¼ cup	butter	50 mL
½ cup	smooth peanut butter	125 mL
4 cups	miniature marshmallows	1 L

1. In a large bowl, combine popped corn, raisins and peanuts. Set aside.

2. In glass measure, combine butter and peanut butter. Microwave, uncovered, on High for 1 to 1½ minutes, stirring once, until melted and smooth.

3. Add marshmallows. Microwave, uncovered, on High for 1½ to 3 minutes, stirring once, until marshmallows are melted. Pour over top of popcorn mixture and mix until well coated.

4. With buttered hands, quickly shape into 3-inch (7.5 cm) balls, pressing firmly so popcorn balls hold their shape. Let cool. Wrap each in plastic wrap.

Micro-Tips

■ Microwave Popcorn: One of the most popular uses of a microwave oven is for popping corn. However, be aware that commercial bags of microwave popcorn now come in several sizes. The popcorn feature of your microwave that automatically programs the time it takes to pop microwave bags of popcorn may be longer than required causing popcorn to burn.

• Never leave popcorn unattended and stop microwaving as soon as you hear the last few kernels popping in the bag to prevent it from scorching.

• Never try to microwave popcorn kernels in a brown paper bag as the bag may ignite and cause an oven fire.

• You can also make popcorn in a microwave popper specifically designed for the microwave. Or use an electrical hot-air popper or pop it conventionally on top of the stove, if desired.

Rocky Road Popcorn

Here's a kid-friendly recipe that is both tasty and easy to make when using a convenient bag of microwave popcorn.

10 cups	freshly popped popcorn (1 bag microwave popcorn, about 3 oz/85 g) (see Micro-Tips, page 183)	2.5 L
½ cup	salted peanuts	125 mL
1½ cups	miniature marshmallows	375 mL
¾ cup	sweet or semisweet chocolate chips	175 mL
¼ cup	peanut butter	50 mL

1. In a large bowl, combine popcorn, peanuts and marshmallows. Set aside.

2. In a microwave-safe bowl, microwave chocolate chips and peanut butter, uncovered, on Medium (50%) for 2 to 3 minutes, stirring often, until melted and smooth.

3. Drizzle half of the sauce over the popcorn mixture and toss to thinly coat. Pour remaining chocolate mixture over top and toss until evenly mixed. Spread popcorn mixture on baking sheet and let stand until cool and chocolate is set. (To hasten cooling, place in refrigerator for about 20 minutes.) Break into chunks to serve.

National Library of Canada Cataloguing in Publication

Burkhard, Johanna
    125 best microwave oven recipes / Johanna Burkhard.

Includes index.
ISBN 0-7788-0092-X

1. Microwave cookery. I. Title. II. Title: One hundred twenty-five best microwave
oven recipes.

TX832.B87 2004   641.5'882   C2003-906397-6

Index

v = variation